BULLET PROOF TRADER

Every owner of a physical copy of this edition of

can download the eBook for free direct from us at Harriman House, in a DRM-free format that can be read on any eReader, tablet or smartphone.

Simply head to:

ebooks.harriman-house.com/bulletprooftrader

to get your copy now.

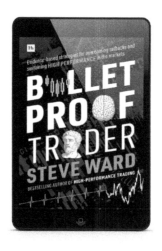

Evidence-based strategies for overcoming setbacks and sustaining **HIGH PERFORMANCE** in the markets

BULLET PROOF TRADER

STEVE WARD

Harriman House

HARRIMAN HOUSE LTD
3 Viceroy Court
Bedford Road
Petersfield
Hampshire
GU32 3LJ
GREAT BRITAIN
Tel: +44 (0)1730 233870

Email: enquiries@harriman-house.com
Website: harriman.house

First published in 2020.
Copyright © Steve Ward

The right of Steve Ward to be identified as the Author has been asserted in accordance with the Copyright, Design and Patents Act 1988.

Paperback ISBN: 978-0-85719-667-5
eBook ISBN: 978-0-85719-668-2

British Library Cataloguing in Publication Data
A CIP catalogue record for this book can be obtained from the British Library.

To Herluf and Merete

CONTENTS

ABOUT
THE AUTHOR

STEVE WARD specialises in helping people working in trading, investing and banking to enhance their risk-taking, improve their decision-making and to achieve and sustain high performance by utilising the latest science, research and practice from performance psychology, decision science, neuroscience, behavioural science, physiology and philosophy.

Since 2005 he has provided specialised coaching, training and consultancy services to traders and fund managers at some of the largest and highest-performing investment banks, hedge funds, asset managers, commodities trading houses, utility companies and proprietary trading groups across the globe.

Prior to starting his work with the financial sector, Steve provided sports psychology coaching to elite athletes and teams in over 30 different sports across the globe, with a particular interest in extreme, action and adventure sports. He has also provided psychological coaching for professional poker players.

Steve is the author of *High-Performance Trading: 35 Practical Strategies and Techniques to Enhance Your Trading Psychology and Performance, Sports Betting to Win: The 10 Keys to Disciplined and Profitable Betting* and *Tradermind: Get a Mindful Edge in the Markets*, and has written many articles for leading trading publications. He co-managed a team of 45 proprietary traders in London, was the consultant trading performance coach to the BBC TV series *Million Dollar Traders*, and spent a number of years trading stock indices and FX on his own account.

performanceedgeconsulting.co.uk

PREFACE: A GUIDE TO THIS BOOK

WHY DO I NEED THIS BOOK?

THIS BOOK IS for any trader who wants to deal with the stresses, emotions, challenges and setbacks encountered while trading the markets – and to trade at their best for the long run.

Any trader knows that trading the markets can be an intensely rewarding pursuit – but by no means a simple or stress-free one. It is possibly one of the most mentally and emotionally challenging activities anyone can pursue. Mistakes, missed opportunites and losses are unavoidable. Stress is frequent and can be intense and protracted. The toll placed on mind, body, behaviour and results can be enormous.

It is possible, however, to harness the insights of psychology, physiology and philosophy – *not* to remove the difficulties of trading, but to navigate them more effectively; and, indeed, to turn them to your advantage. This has been one of the key areas of focus in my work with traders and investors across the globe, at every level of experience, and across all markets over the last 15 years. The ability to manage the psychological and physiological challenges of trading the markets is key to performing at your best and maximising market returns.

This is not my first book on trading performance. *High-Performance Trading* remains, I hope, a helpful collection of practical, bite-sized strategies for improving any trader's psychology – a kind of manual of exercises you can dip in and out of at need. *Tradermind* provides mindfulness-based approaches.

The goal of *Bulletproof Trader* is to offer a practical resource for traders to help them deal with the mental, emotional and physical challenges and demands of trading the markets. It is also a chance to share the latest insights from research and practice on the ground, including:

- the fascinating realm of biofeedback — objective measures of how the market influences a trader's physiology (and vice versa)

- the latest 'third wave' of psychological techniques

- practical approaches grounded in ancient performance philosophy.

All these have informed my work with my clients over the past few years.

There is nothing more rewarding, in my experience, than helping people reach their full potential in a dynamic and challenging pursuit like trading. But of course no coach can work with every trader around the world. This book allows me to be a resource for you, and share what I have seen help many other traders.

DO I NEED TO BE A PARTICULAR KIND OF TRADER?

You don't need to be a particular kind of trader to benefit from this book.

I have worked with traders from across the globe, from beginner to higly experienced and successful 'Market Wizards', trading every kind of market and strategy. This book is written to be relevant to all of them.

It is also, I believe, relevant to investors. They may not face emotional or psychological challenges with quite the same intensity and regularity – after all, they are not entering and exiting the market with the same frequency – but the experience is not entirely dissimilar. Especially in down times, or moments of volatility; and the times we are living in have not been lacking in those.

HOW IS THE BOOK STRUCTURED?

This book is built around nine parts, with 25 chapters in total. We'll start by laying the foundations of bulletproof trading in the first couple of chapters, before building on that with specific strategies and techniques to help you:

- take committed action
- identify your values and who you want to be as a trader
- manage your risk
- embrace uncertainty
- plan for (and therefore beat) the worst
- train your attention and awareness
- focus on your trading process
- control the controllables

- get comfortable with being uncomfortable

- unhook from difficult thoughts

- work with stress-based emotions

- build confidence in coping with difficult trading situations

- stay calm in critical market moments

- avoid beating yourself up

- find the opportunity in the difficult, and turn adversity into advantage

- get good at adapting to change in the markets

- monitor your stress and fatigue levels

- master the art of recovery to build resilience and sustain performance

- develop your physiological fitness and toughness.

I have tried to make the book practical throughout, with numerous exercises both to explain the concepts and to help you develop the mental, emotional and physical skills of a bulletproof trader. These exercises, and the techniques taught within the book, are evidence-based and the same ones I use with my own trading and investing clients.

While I appreciate it is often easy to skip over exercises and activities when reading a book, I strongly recommend that you take the time to complete and practise them as best as possible to get the full benefits of *Bulletproof Trader*.

PART ONE

BECOMING BULLETPROOF

1

WHY BULLETPROOF?

"I want to bulletproof myself."

T'S SEPTEMBER 2014 and I'm sitting in the boardroom of a hedge fund in the West End of London having a one-to-one coaching meeting with a new client, the hedge fund's founder. He's a successful trader with an incredible track record going back many years. I'm dressed in my standard uniform of casual trousers and shirt. Across the table he sits in shorts and polo shirt, notepad and pen at the ready.

After an exchange of initial pleasantries – primarily a discussion about the weekend's football results – I prepare to ask my first question. I am aiming to find out more about the trader, his key biographical details, trading history, trading style and strategy – and what outcomes he would like to see from the coaching programme.

"What do you want to achieve?" I ask.

"To be able to deal with my trading performance and results with greater equanimity," he replies.

"And why now?" I ask.

"I have never really had an extended run of bad performance. But I know that statistically one is likely to happen. I have to prepare myself for that. I need to make sure I have the skills to handle such an event. I want to bulletproof myself."

"How would you know if you were… bulletproof?" I said. I hadn't heard that phrase used like that before. It stuck with me.

"I would have fewer negative thoughts," he said. "I can get obsessed about decisions I have made, especially when I have lost money or am not making it. I can be a perfectionistic. When I fail, I can't stop thinking about it, and I know that mindset is not helpful. Sometimes I am just sat there telling myself 'what a f****** idiot' over and over again. My emotions can be very negative. Sometimes I feel pretty depressed. Trading can make me feel sick."

"And what would be the benefits of being bulletproof?"

"Ultimately I think it is about keeping me in the game. I love what I do, and want to be doing this for many years. I don't want a big negative event to take me out. But I would like to be able to change some of my thinking and how I feel when things are not going well."

We went on to define in greater depth what being 'bulletproof' meant for him – identifying particular situations where it would be useful and looking at what bulletproof behaviours might be. We explored some tough situations he had already faced in his trading career and overcome. It was important to discover his current level of bulletproofing. Any trader or fund manager who has traded the markets for a long period of time will have developed a certain level of resiliency to still be in his or her seat trading – even if they feel they're currently in crisis.

Over the next 12 months I helped this top trader develop a range of strategies that increased his ability to deal with tough trading situations. We were 'lucky' in that during our work together there were a couple of significant market events that had a big negative impact on his results – and provided great opportunities to practise what we had been working on together.

Our work included:

- learning about the importance of anticipating and planning ahead for challenges
- the power of acceptance (of your situation and your *experience* of that situation)
- how to manage the mind and the emotion-driven thoughts than can arise in times of difficulty
- understanding perception – and how the way we see a situation creates our reaction or response to that situation
- being able to see the opportunity within a challenge
- being comfortable with the worst-case scenario.

We also undertook some simple mindfulness-based meditation practices to increase in-the-moment awareness, gain greater objectivity, lower emotional reactivity and increase equanimity.

Lastly, we spent some time using biofeedback. This involved learning techniques for increasing the strength of his nervous system, making him less reactive to doses of stress – particularly the impact of it on his decision-making.

All in all, he developed an extensive toolkit that robustly increased his level of bulletproofing. Importantly, he worked at using the tools provided – he practised the skills – and as a result attained a level of trading resilience beyond his initial expectations.

A key part of this is because he spent time and energy developing the skills to become more bulletproof. I believe this is something any trader can do.

COACHING TRADERS

I have been fortunate enough to spend the last 15 years coaching and training thousands of traders and fund managers across the globe at banks, funds, commodities trading houses, asset managers, proprietary trading groups, utility companies – as well as individuals trading from home.

I would summarise my role as helping my clients to trade at their best.

To do this I provide coaching, training and advice around risk-taking, decision-making, and achieving and sustaining high performance. I draw on research and practice from psychology, physiology, behavioural science, neuroscience, peak performance, decision science and – most recently – philosophy. All the while, I try to stay mindful of *what actually works* with real traders in real markets.

The result is a blending of the science of performance with the art of coaching.

Some clients, around 20–30% or so, come to me because they are performing well and want to sustain that level over time, or to move up to the next level, to stretch themselves in the pursuit of becoming their best trading self.

The vast majority seek support, however, because they are facing a challenge of some kind in the markets – a drop or stagnation in results, some psychological discomfort (thoughts or feelings) or an uncomfortable physiological response (stress or fatigue).

This imbalance reflects a number of factors: firstly, human nature, and our negativity bias. Secondly, how reactive traders are to their P&L, especially the 'L' part of that. Thirdly, how challenging and demanding trading the markets is psychologically and physiologically.

TOUGH TIMES

Pre-2008 a great deal of my work in trading and investing was framed around maximising returns, increasing performance – going from good to great.

There was a growing sense that trading and investing psychology was creating a performance edge, and an increasing number of traders and fund managers were exploring its possibilities. Post-financial crisis, that focus on performance enhancement continued, but another theme came to prominence: managing stress, performing under pressure, dealing with setbacks, coping with challenges and change, sustaining performance.

In other words, resilience.

This has only increased in the years since. Redundancies, regulatory changes, reduced head counts, sustained or increased targets and budgets (with less resources), information overload, new technology, market structure changes and evolutions, not to mention a global pandemic and many of the above coming together all at the same time (a "cluster f***" as one head of desk at a bank described it to me) have placed huge demands on traders.

SUPPORT, SKILLS AND STRATEGIES

For some traders I have worked with, the challenges they've faced have been relatively short-term and situational. For others they have been longer and more drawn out.

For both types of trader, my role as a coach has been twofold.

Firstly, to support them – to be a person they can confide in. Someone they can talk about their challenges with; someone they can reflect on things with. Someone who can advise and guide as required.

Secondly, to help them to develop specific mental, emotional and physical skills and strategies that enable them to overcome the challenges they are facing – and which will also be valuable additional tools in their psychological and physiological armoury going forward.

I hope that this book can provide you with the second of these, as a way of helping you to develop your own bulletproofing skills.

WHAT BRINGS YOU HERE?

Whenever I take an enquiry from a trader or an institution about working together, I like to understand what has led them to getting in touch.

Some examples of what brings traders to my coaching include:

- New traders at the start of their careers looking for support in developing a resilient mindset and the mental skills required to deal with the challenges of trading the markets.

- Experiencing a large loss and seeking help to deal with the experience – and to recover effectively.

- Being in a period of drawdown/losses and wanting support in getting through it.

- Lacking in confidence; being unable to pull the trigger on trades or to take the level of risk they feel they could or should be taking.

- Needing support with managing a change of some type, perhaps in trading style or in trading a new product.

- Managing the demands of trading and the demands of life *outside* trading.

- Help with developing composure to manage big moments in the markets.

- Learning to become more comfortable with the uncertainty and ambiguity of the markets.

- Managing emotions such as fear, anger, frustration, regret and anxiety.

- Strengthening discipline, or consistency, of trade execution.

- Help with managing physical energy – reducing fatigue, overcoming exhaustion and burnout.

- Managing impatience, dealing with quieter and slower-moving markets, overcoming boredom trading or reducing overtrading.

- Struggling with being wrong, with losing money or making mistakes.

- Finding it hard to stay in winning trades, running winners.

Before you read further, my question to you is: what brings *you* here?

Is there a particular reason you are reading this book? What would you like to get out of it?

2

THE BULLETPROOF FRAMEWORK

THE KEY REQUIREMENTS

I AM OFTEN ASKED what I believe are the key requirements for becoming a successful trader. One thing that I would say is absolutely critical is the ability to manage the highs and lows – but especially the lows.

That ability might be termed 'resilience', 'mental toughness' or 'stress-hardiness', but for this book I am borrowing the term *bulletproof* from my hedge fund client we met in chapter 1.

> "Success comes to the lowly and to the poorly talented, but the special characteristic of a great person is to triumph over the disasters and panics of human life."
>
> **– Seneca**

THE FOUR FOUNDATIONS OF BULLETPROOF TRADING

The ability to perform under stress and pressure, to cope with the highs and lows of performance in high-stakes environments, has been thoroughly researched over the years. Traders are now able to benefit from the findings – and practice – of the military, elite athletes, law enforcement and performing artists. All of which feed into this book.

When it comes to helping my trading clients develop their ability to manage the challenges and difficulties of trading, my work is influenced by many different areas of study. They can be grouped broadly under the headings of *psychology*, *physiology*, *philosophy* and the all-important fourth component, *pragmatism*. I believe that a multidisciplinary approach is required to maximise trading performance, and to become a bulletproof trader.

The Bulletproof Trader framework

1. PSYCHOLOGY

Trading psychology draws on a broad field of research and practice, including decision science, behavioural finance, performance psychology, cognitive psychology and more. In this book, you will see input from all of these areas. But I have focused much of the psychological framework on contextual behavioural science and the development of *psychological flexibility*.

Developing psychological flexibility is the goal of Acceptance Commitment Coaching, a derivative of Acceptance Commitment Therapy or ACT (pronounced as 'act' not A.C.T.) which was originally developed by University of Nevada psychologist Steven C. Hayes. ACT is third-wave cognitive psychology. It is distinct from other cognitive approaches, such as cognitive behavioural therapy, in that its fundamental goal is not to change or control unwanted thoughts, emotions or sensations, but rather to be aware of them, and accept them, while keeping a strong focus on action.

Rather than focusing on the specific content of your thoughts and emotions, ACT is more focused on the context you are in, and the function (helpfulness or workability) of your behaviour in a specific context – as well as how you are relating to your thoughts, emotions, sensations and urges.

ACT-based approaches have helped people improve their performance in sports, chess and in music, and at work,[1] including alleviating stress and increasing resilience. ACT is a core part of my trading psychology model. I believe that the development of psychological flexibility has a very positive impact on traders' ability to stay focused on their trading process. It helps them manage the thoughts, emotions, sensations and urges that can cause them to drift from their process.

Alongside a focus on the development of psychological flexibility, I have drawn on the research and practice of developing stress hardiness[2] and mental toughness.[3] Specifically, on these core factors:

- **Commitment** – having a sense of purpose for why you are doing what you are doing, and being disciplined and dedicated to taking action.

- **Control** – largely centred around a person's locus of control, whether internal or external; whether people believe they can influence how they respond to events or not. Being able to identify what you can and can't control is a key skill.

- **Challenge** – seeing change events as opportunities to grow, and being willing to work through challenges and difficulty.

- **Confidence** – feeling you can cope with difficulty and setbacks, and seeing and seizing opportunity.

2. PHYSIOLOGY

An important part of the bulletproof framework is the role that our *physiology* plays in our ability to perform under stress.

At the physiological level there are some key areas that traders can really benefit from, including:

- being able to recognise shifts in your physiology (e.g. breathing, heart rate) as indicators of a shift in your body's physical state – stress response and energy levels in particular

- recognising the need to regulate the stress response when it is too high and potentially impacting your decision-making

- learning strategies to develop your physiological resilience to the stress response – increasing your stress capacity

- managing your stress vs recovery balance so that you can strengthen your physiology muscles, reduce fatigue and sustain high performance over time.

3. PHILOSOPHY

While writing this book I became increasingly interested in the philosophy and practices of Stoicism and its potential application to helping traders deal with the challenges they face in trading the markets.

Stoicism was founded in Greece by Zeno of Citium (Cyprus today) in the early third-century BC. Zeno was a merchant who lost everything in a shipwreck and turned to philosophy in order to rebuild his life, and later taught his messages in a *stoa* (covered walkway), where his school became known as the Stoa and from where Stoicism gets its name.

I first came across the benefits of applying Stoicism to my work with traders after reading Ryan Holiday's *The Obstacle is the Way*,[4] a book that took the 2,000-year-old Stoic principles and practices and set them into a modern-day text, aimed at helping people to "turn adversity into advantage". This book has become a popular read for athletes and coaches, and for people operating in competitive or high-stakes environments.

In an article discussing Stoicism in the NFL, Holiday states: "Stoicism as a philosophy is really about the mental game. It's not a set of ethics or principles. It's a collection of spiritual exercises designed to help people through the difficulty of life."[5]

For many people, the word 'stoic' suggests being unemotional in the face of adversity. This is a modern and inaccurate misinterpretation. The Stoics were *not* in favour of being emotionless, but they certainly *were* in favour of finding ways to manage and reduce the impact of unhelpful emotions.

Stoicism, at its core, is a robust and highly practical action-orientated philosophy that aims to help people develop the skills to manage the struggles of life. It encourages you to focus your thoughts and actions *on that which you can control*. If you cannot control something, you have to accept it. The key is to take responsibility for how you respond – and to express your best self in every moment.

This is essential, and very powerful, for traders.

4. PRAGMATISM

Alongside the science it is important that the strategies in this book actually work with real traders in real trading environments. Research is important and interesting but the real-world trading floor is the true testing ground of effectiveness.

All of the techniques and strategies in this book have been used successfully with my own clients – thousands of traders and fund managers – and the wider trading, investing and banking performance communities, such as sales and research.

Their feedback has been invaluable in shaping the content. Where possible I have shared it, as well as providing example case studies to show this real-world application.

GETTING THE MOST FROM THIS BOOK

This book has been written to be a practical resource rather than a scientific text. There are numerous exercises and activities throughout. Completing them will help maximise the impact of the book on your trading performance.

I know that this is not always easy. The key is to start by perhaps focusing on one or two areas where you would really like to benefit. Initially, you can commit to taking action in *just those areas*. That will make a significant difference to you and your trading, and will make further changes easier.

You can read and learn as much about running mechanics and training theory as you like, but to get better at running you actually have to do some running.

Action is at the core of performance.

"That's why the philosophers warn us not to be satisfied with mere learning, but to add practice and then training. For, as time passes, we forget what we learned and end up doing the opposite and hold opinions the opposite of what we should."

– Epictetus

Stay open-minded and maintain a sense of curiosity; adopt an 'experimental' mindset when it comes to applying the strategies and techniques here. I have been involved in the field of performance enhancement for many years and I see it as very much about self-experimentation.

You get a hunch about something that might help you improve your trading. You test it, adapt it, refine it – or bin it if doesn't work, and try something different.

A FUTURE BULLETPROOF TRADER: YOU

You will already be bulletproof to some extent, thanks to a combination of life and trading experiences. Much of what you are already doing may well be very helpful. This book does not aim to replace that. But even in areas where things are going well, I would encourage you to read with an eye to opportunities to try new approaches.

What got you *here* may not get you *there*.

Imagine for a moment a future trading you: even more resilient and capable of handling the challenges and demands that you face in trading the markets. What would be different? What would you notice? What action would you be taking? How would you be feeling? What thoughts would you have?

Where are the opportunities for you to develop, to become a mentally stronger, more robust, composed and resilient trader than you currently are?

TRAINING YOUR MIND TO ADAPT TO ANY CIRCUMSTANCE

It took me a long time to finalise and organise the content of this book, and just as perfectionism is a dangerous trait in trading it can be equally debilitating in writing. But my intention is not to tell you what to do, but rather to help you to develop a framework: the skills and practices – mental, emotional and physical – that are most relevant and powerful for your trading.

That is what will truly help you meet the challenges and demands of trading the markets as they arise.

"In this way you must understand how laughable it is to say, 'Tell
me what to do!' What advice could I possibly give? No, a far
better request is, 'Train my mind to adapt to any circumstance'...
In this way if circumstances take you off script you won't be
desperate for a new prompting."

– Epictetus

Each trader is like each moment in the market: unique. And
what works for one person may not work for another. As you
read through the book, I encourage you to keep reflecting on
the question:

* 'Could this be helpful for me in my own trading? And if so,
  when and how can I apply it?'

PART TWO

UPS AND DOWNS

3

THE NATURE
OF TRADING

Before you get into this chapter, take a few moments to reflect on these two questions:

- What are the challenges and demands you face in trading the markets?

- What do you need to be good at in order to meet those challenges and demands?

TRADING AS A HIGH-PERFORMANCE ACTIVITY

I T WAS FEBRUARY 2005 when I first stepped onto a trading floor. It was the first Friday of the month, non-farm payrolls day (the release of US employment data – as I later found out, a significant day and a big market opportunity for traders).

I can remember the minutes leading up to the data release so clearly. The traders – well over 100 in total – all returned to their seats and began to prepare themselves for the upcoming announcement. Then came the countdown from the in-house analyst – "one minute"… the noise and hustle on the floor died down… "thirty seconds"… a focused hush… "ten seconds"… a feeling of anticipation, expectation, an obvious increase in adrenaline and energy… "five seconds"…

Then the data was read over the squawk box. There was an eruption of activity, noise, emotion. It was visible even within a few seconds that many traders were experiencing high levels of stress – and the emotions that came with it.

Over the coming hours I witnessed the highs and lows that trading the markets can bring. Some of the traders made large sums of money, others were flat, some were seriously down and nursing big losses on the day. It was my first encounter with trading. I became acutely aware that trading was a challenging, pressurised and often stressful occupation – something that only became more vivid as I spent time working with traders.

And I recognised that challenge, pressure and stress from another world entirely.

Before working with traders, I had spent a number of years as a sports psychology coach to elite athletes and teams. Trading was undoubtedly the nearest activity to sport that wasn't a sport. Like elite sport, trading is a high-performance activity – and makes for a demanding environment in which traders must operate.

THE TRADING PERFORMANCE ENVIRONMENT

One of the core demands in trading is making risk-based decisions under conditions of uncertainty. Both risk and uncertainty are *stressors*. That is, they activate the stress response in our nervous system. The work of behavioural finance and neuropsychology shows clear challenges for the brain in making decisions under such conditions.

Humans prefer comfort, certainty, familiarity. A sense of control. Traders are continually exposed to a lack of control over market conditions and the outcomes they get on any given trade. Each trading decision has consequences and those consequences must be dealt with, not only financially but psychologically and physiologically. Traders must cope with the highs and lows of winning and losing – with strings of losses, with making mistakes, with being wrong, even with getting a bad outcome from a good process.

You did all the right things, prepared well, executed well, managed your risk, stayed flexible, yet still lost.

Often, decisions are made with incomplete information, sometimes within short time frames – both of these take further cognitive and emotional tolls. For those traders working within institutions there are the added pressures of making your budget for the year and servicing clients; for fund managers, the additional challenges of dealing with investors and the potential of redemptions.

The trader's performance environment

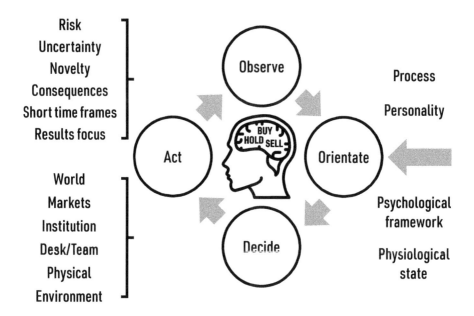

UPS AND DOWNS

"When you are making money trading is the best job in the world.
When you are losing money it is the worst."

– A futures trader

It is common for me to arrive on the trading floor and to greet traders informally with a *'How's things?'* and to be met by the phrase *'Ups and downs'*, or in more severe cases, *'Ups and downs, but mainly downs'*.

That response, more than anything else, summarises the trading experience. For some shorter-time-frame traders these ups and downs occur multiple times over the course of the trading day. For others they may be less frequent or more protracted.

I have never met a trader who experienced any other version of events than *ups and downs*.

In fact, in over 20 years of working with elite performers across a range of high-performance domains I always heard the same story. I believe it is common to all high performers pursuing performance excellence. It's a consequence of choosing to take up challenging activities, performed in demanding environments. And it's a result of caring about what you do.

If you want low stress, the simplest strategy is not to give a s***. The downside is you probably won't achieve your best results.

These ups and downs define the whole trading experience – the *journey*. It is through the downs that we develop the attitude and skills that prepare us for future challenges.

Of course, life itself is full of 'ups and downs'. Trading the markets is ultimately just a highly concentrated form of the human experience. And we are wired for survival – which is both what gives rise to difficult thoughts, emotions and sensations. And what means we can ultimately overcome them.

> "Life is hard, brutal, punishing, narrow, confusing, a deadly business."
> – Epictetus

The downs of trading can be momentary – or they can be protracted. Traders need the skills to manage both. Stress can be a short-term 'acute' response, or 'chronic', a longer-term exposure. Chronic stress brings with it an additional challenge for traders, one which I have had plenty of experience of with my own clients: fatigue and exhaustion, at the extreme end of which lies burnout.

Stress and fatigue play a huge part in reducing a trader's ability to make good decisions and perform at their best. They bias traders towards the short term, amplify risk aversion, increase bias-proneness and reduce cognitive functions such as self-control. Building the resources to offset the stress response and reduce fatigue, to increase physiological capacity, is fundamental to being bulletproof.

The psychobiology of winning runs and losing runs

	Winning run	Losing run
Brain	Reward-seeking circuits activated	Risk-avoidance circuits activated
Hormone	Testosterone	Cortisol
Emotion	Excitement	Fear
Feeling	Pleasure	Pain
Risk	Risk seeking	Risk aversion
Bias	Overconfidence, irrational exuberance	Underconfidence, irrational pessimism

A survey of my trading clients revealed a variety of examples of the stressors that traders face. I have listed them below, and for a few have given the feedback in the trader's own words. Which of these ring true for you?

• Dealing with losses and drawdown.

> "July–Aug 2017 I lost my whole year's P&L from a series of absurdly over-exposed positions. I didn't deal with it very well. At all."

• Uncertainty in the markets.
• Volatility.
• Missing out on trades.

> "I cannot stand when the market does the 'most obvious thing' and I don't have the position on or am the wrong way round through overthinking it."

> "Seeing other people do well in a consensus move and being the other way has caused me to trade out of frustration and anger initially; then panic when it continues to go against me."

- Expectations, pressure.
- Worrying about how to make money, where the next P&L will come from.

> "I get wound up not so much by what my current year-to-date P&L is, but more the feeling of 'where is my next $ going to come from'? After having a series of losing trades/days/weeks, I begin to think how am I possibly going to make another $ from this? I've had moments where I am flat or down on the year, but have felt incredible optimism because I think I am onto the right strategy going forward. Same in reverse; had great half years then hit a bad patch and thought to myself: I literally have no ideas left and I can't see how it's even possible for me to add to my YTD numbers."

- Being wrong.
- Taking heat on a position, being offside.

> "When I have a relatively large position and am heavily offside, this can distract me from other opportunities as I'm so focused on the position that's concerning me."

- Being behind budget/target for the year.
- Other people's results being better than yours.
- Quiet markets, boredom.

> "No market action and the anticipation of signals that haven't manifested yet – here the main problem for me is to deal with the impatience affecting my decision-making process."

- Holding overnight positions.
- Major risk events.

> "My most stressful trading situations have been big major risk events like Brexit, major European elections, etc. Mainly due to the fact that due to the increased volatility you have a level expectation on yourself of how well you should be doing – and so, regardless of how you do, you tend to feel you should have done better."

- Investor redemptions.
- Not being able to execute trades as you would like to, liquidity.

> "During a drawdown, wanting to reduce position sizes, but not being able to – this is a real problem in credit markets where liquidity (your ability to buy or, more importantly, sell an asset) can disappear in an instant. Knowing what trades you want to do, and not being able to do them, is a more stressful experience than the loss."

- Regulation.
- Making a mistake.
- Large positions.
- Multiple positions in the market.

> "Most stressful situations for me tend to arise when I am trading either too much size or too many products at one time."

- Management and leadership 'interference'.

- Career risk.

- Balancing trading and life commitments.

> "Outside of risk-specific stressful events I would say the next most challenging experience I have is the constant battle with balanced intensity, with my commitments outside of trading; and then trying to manage my own trading book through various periods of increased volatility often brings frustrations and distractions that result in poor performance across the board."

- Overload of information.

- External distractions.

- Fatigue, exhaustion and burnout.

That's a very extensive list of stressors that traders face. It illustrates the complex nature of the trading environment. Not every trader will experience all of these, of course; everyone's stress response is individual. But these are, in my experience, representative – and the kinds of stressor I have focused on helping you deal with in this book.

These situations require traders to have the psychological skills and physiological capacity to overcome them and trade at their best.

4

GET GOOD AT THE DOWNS

THE PAIN OF LOSS

IMAGINE YOU HAVE been invited to take a bet on a coin toss – heads or tails. If you call incorrectly you lose $100. How much would you want to win, if correct, in order to take the bet?

This is a question from research in behavioural finance that I often ask in my trading psychology workshops. The most popular answers are between $101 and $300 (the market makers, scalpers and high-frequency traders looking for multiple plays at the $101 end of the spectrum; the directional traders with their 2:1 or 3:1 risk-reward ratios at the $200–300 end).

Occasionally a few people come in at around $500, with the odd person at $1,000.

Research into loss aversion suggests that, in the example above, on average people want to win around $200.[6] That is, they would like $200 to offset the risk of losing $100, such that $2 of pleasure is needed to offset every $1 of pain.

Flipped around: the pain of loss is twice the pleasure of winning.

This asymmetric relationship between the pleasure of winning and the pain of losing, in combination with our brain's bias towards negativity (hence the strength of our stress-based survival emotions) goes some way to explaining why the downs of trading can feel so painful.

It is important that we find a way to deal with this pain.

I was recently having a coffee with a trader I coached many years ago who has now left trading. We were talking about how amazing trading and life was when he was making money ("You almost feel invincible"), and how tough it could be when it was not going well. He went on to tell me that there had been several times in his career when he had been really struggling with his trading – and much worse than I knew.

He had been losing money, losing confidence, losing self-belief. And on his commute home he had stood on the train platform and thought: *'What would it be like if I jumped. Would it be quick?'*

Trading as a craft is challenging to master, but a trader also needs to master his or her mind and body. Becoming bulletproof is about being able to survive the short-term stresses of trading and to stay in the game for the long term.

I have sometimes heard people refer to trading the markets as a dance. In reality it is more like a wrestling match. A dance partner is not likely to get up and tackle you to the floor, or put you in a choke hold to make you submit.

> "The art of living is more like wrestling than dancing, because an artful life involves being prepared to meet and withstand sudden and unexpected attacks."
>
> – Marcus Aurelius

THE INNER CITADEL

"I have on two occasions lost my whole year in short spaces of time.
One being as a very inexperienced, naive trader where I had left
excessive orders in a market overnight and a pipeline burst and
caused the market to spike, resulting in me waking up in the morning
to a large short position and my year's work gone. The other was as
a more experienced trader and being stubborn, and over-confident in
my positions and really not managing my risk well. The second time
was a far bigger monetary hit but also a lot harder as I had very high
hopes for that year and was on cloud nine... this hit took me back
down to earth and made me realise what markets are capable of
doing. They were both humbling experiences."

– A commodities trader

Are you mentally prepared for the challenges and difficulties of trading?

Do you have a mental framework to deal with losses, making mistakes, missing out on opportunities, fear, anxiety, uncertainty, stress, drawdown, redemptions, change, poor results?

There is no shame in answering 'no' at this stage. Being ready for dealing with such adversity is not something we are born with, it is developed throughout our life and through our life experiences – it is forged.

The Stoics recognised the need to be prepared for adversity and developed a philosophy – a way of thinking and, importantly, *doing* – that was focused on preparing and fortifying them for challenges to come. In many ways these ancient philosophers were like mental athletes, developing their mental strength, flexibility and stamina ready to face the challenges of life.

They talked about the "Inner Citadel" – "the fortress inside of you that no external adversity could ever break down".[7]

I think of the inner citadel as a mental fortress – built up by skills and practices that allow you to manage adversity effectively. This fortress is not there at birth. It is established through your life and your trading experiences. Part of becoming bulletproof is building and strengthening your inner citadel. Within this book, each exercise and technique is an opportunity to add another stone to your fortress walls.

Ask yourself:

- How is your inner citadel currently?

- How are you already working on building your inner fortress?

GETTING GOOD AT THE DOWNS

You cannot remove the risk from trading. That means that negative experiences are part of the game. They are inherent to the nature of the activity. All traders experience stress, difficult thoughts, unwanted emotions and uncomfortable sensations at times. When you make a trade you are taking a risk; it is perfectly natural to feel some stress.

The goal is to get good at dealing with the stress – with the downs. The most effective way that you begin to learn to deal with tough trading situations is by being in them.

It is being in loss-making trades, enduring periods of drawdown, recovering from a mistake, missing out on an opportunity, experiencing fear and dealing with changing market conditions where you develop your coping skills and strategies. It is through exposure to stressful events that you train your physiology to endure the physical responses to stress.

If you avoid stressful or difficult situations in your trading you never develop the psychological or physiological capacity to deal with them and achieve your trading potential.

> " 'No tree becomes deep rooted unless strong winds blow against it' – the shaking and pulling is what makes the tree tighten its grip and plant its roots more securely – heavy rain and strong winds are to the advantage of good people."[8]

The goal in becoming bulletproof is not to avoid or get rid of trading stress or discomfort. The goal is to get good at it.

Take a moment to think of times in your trading (or in a life event, if that is more useful), when you:

- overcame a difficult period

- bounced back from a tough situation, setback or loss

- got through a difficult time with relative ease

- challenged yourself on purpose and went out of your comfort zone.

For each situation, ask yourself the following questions:

- How did you get through it?

- What characteristics, strengths or attitudes did you demonstrate?

- What skills did you use?

- What lessons did you learn?

This exercise is a great reminder of the experiential nature of becoming bulletproof. It's why we're going to be action-focused rather than avoidance-orientated in our work on improving your trading.

"What would have become of Hercules, do you think, if there had been no lion, hydra, stag or boar – and no savage criminals to rid the world of? What would he have done in the absence of such challenges?"

– Epictetus

PART
THREE

COMMITMENT

5

MINDSET OVER MATTER

YOUR TRADING MINDSET

"It is our attitude toward events, not events themselves, which we can control. Nothing is by its own nature calamitous – even death is terrible only if we fear it."

– Epictetus

Y OUR MINDSET IS a collection of your beliefs, perceptions and rules. It reflects how you think about yourself, the world and others. It also shapes how you think about things. In trading, your mindset will define (and be defined by) how you think about vital factors such as the markets, risk, uncertainty, money, winning, losing and mistakes.

The role of mindset in your trading experience

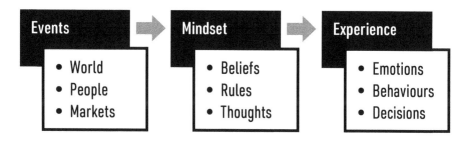

Your mindset develops from birth and is influenced by the experiences and environments you encounter. It's affected by your family, schooling, life, friendship groups, sports and hobbies, further education and work. From the moment you start reading about trading, learning how to trade, or getting exposed to the markets – your trading mindset is developing.

Key events and people, both positive and negative, can play a significant role in shaping your mindset for the better. A financial crisis, a tough period of drawdown – as much as a winning run, a respected colleague or a good coach or mentor – can all help you develop beliefs and perceptions that support your best trading performance.

But while some aspects of your mindset will be helpful, others will be unhelpful, taking you away from the trading actions required for maximising your chances of success.

One of the aspects of becoming a bulletproof trader is developing a mindset that supports successful trading. This is something that will surface throughout the book, but the focus here is mainly on our mindset and its approach to *stress and setbacks*.

How you think about stress – and the challenges, setbacks, losses and mistakes that give rise to it – will profoundly impact your experience and success in the markets.

GETTING GOOD AT STRESS

Health psychologist Kelly McGonigal writes in her book *The Upside of Stress* about the importance of *getting good at stress* rather than avoiding it.[9] She cites some interesting research which looked at people's perception of stress and its impact on their health. The study asked 28,000 adults over an eight-year period to rate their perceived levels of stress over the previous year, whether they believed stress was harmful or not, and what actions they took to control their stress.

People who had experienced high stress and who also believed that stress had affected their health had a 43% increased chance of premature death.

By contrast, people who had stated they had experienced high levels of stress *but that stress was not harmful to their health* had the lowest risk of dying, even lower than those who had low stress but believed their stress was harmful.

The key outcome from this research challenges the belief that it is stress *per se* that is bad for us. That doesn't seem to be the case. Nor is it the amount of stress that causes problems to our health. Rather, it is our belief about whether stress is harmful or not – what our *perception* of stress is.

It is our mindset about stress that matters most.

In another study reported in the book, people were put through two stressful situations: a five-minute videotaped speech on their personal weaknesses in front of a panel trained to actively unsettle them, followed by a maths test where they had to count backwards from 996 in sevens, again in front of a panel who provided unsettling feedback.

Before the tests, some people in the study group were told that the feelings of stress in such situations, and the physical responses they might experience (e.g. increased heart rate and quicker breathing), would be helpful. They were your body's way of preparing you for the challenge at hand, enabling you to perform at your best. As a result of this instruction these participants performed more effectively and with a lower level of stress, compared to those members of the study who were told that the feelings and sensations of stress in such a situation were harmful to performance.

It appears that what we think about stress has more impact on our bodies, our health, and on our performance than the actual stress itself. With this in mind, one of the most important strategies for managing your trading stress is to change how you think about it.

Traders need to see that stress is both normal and – importantly – can be helpful. This reduces the impact of stress on your health in the long term (chronic stress), and may also increase your trading performance in the short term (acute stress).

Two steps to developing a performance-enhancing mindset around stress are:

1. Accept the inherent stresses of trading the market.

2. See the stress response as helpful and performance-enhancing.

LOSSES, MISTAKES AND SETBACKS

What is your mindset around losing, failure and mistakes?

In his book *Black Box Thinking*, which examines the role that failure plays in success, Matthew Syed contrasts the culture surrounding mistakes and failure in the medicine and aviation industries.[10]

In medicine he finds there has historically been a negative culture around mistakes, with low reporting levels, influenced perhaps by the motivation to avoid being sued for medical negligence. The outcome of this culture is that mistakes are made *but people don't learn from them*. So the same mistakes are repeated and performance doesn't improve.

By contrast, he finds a much more open culture around mistakes in aviation. Here mistakes are reported and shared, not just within airlines, but across different airlines around the world, allowing a pervasive learning from those mistakes. Everybody can benefit – and safety levels and performance are improved across the industry.

What is your own internal culture around mistakes? Around losses, setbacks and difficulty?

Ray Dalio of Bridgewater Capital strongly believes that learning from mistakes is essential to improvement and ultimate success.[11] He suggests that each mistake, if recognised and acted on, provides an opportunity for improving your trading. Traders can benefit from writing down the mistake, the implied lesson and the intended change (if required) to their trading process. This log can then be reviewed for reinforcement. Trading mistakes cannot be completely avoided – but repeating the same mistake can be.

Developing a mindset that enables you to see mistakes, setbacks and losses as opportunities to develop as a trader can be very helpful in helping you to manage them more effectively.

The Stoics were strong believers that challenges and setbacks were a part of life and important opportunities for self-improvement. Their philosophy developed a mindset that saw adversity as an advantage, and obstacles as the way.

> "Our actions may be impeded, but there can be no impeding our intentions or dispositions. Because we can accommodate and adapt. The mind adapts and converts to its own purpose the obstacle for our acting. The impediment to action advances action. What stands in the way becomes the way."
>
> **– Marcus Aurelius**

This same mindset can be very helpful for traders.

A three-step process for managing and learning from your trading losses, mistakes and setbacks could be:

1. See losses, mistakes and setbacks as opportunities to learn.

2. Write down how you are thinking and feeling about a given loss/mistake/setback.

3. Write down the lesson(s) from the loss/mistake/setback and any action you will take as a result in the future.

A WORTHY RIVAL

When I worked as a sports psychology coach, I encountered some athletes who developed anxieties about facing a certain opponent; often one who was more highly ranked or regarded as a better performer, more likely to win.

Some of these athletes became truly fearful of facing these opponents. They tried to avoid it at all costs. In the short term this avoidance of the opponent reduced their anxieties. But in the long term they lost out on the opportunity to play better opponents, to develop and raise their own game, and become a better performer.

In order to help these athletes I encouraged a mindset shift from fearing playing tougher opponents to *actively seeking them out.* I would remind them of the meaning of the word competition. In its Latin root it comes from a combination of *com* meaning 'together', and *petere* meaning 'to seek' – giving an original meaning of 'to seek together'.

There was no element of winning or losing.

I helped them build a mindset that appreciated that competitive encounters were opportunities for the players involved to 'seek together' – to find ways of developing and becoming better at their craft, at managing their minds and honing their bodies. The best opportunities to do so were when your competitor was a tough one, a better player, someone who would test you; someone you would train hard to prepare for, and who would create opportunities for you to develop your game.

These opponents were *worthy rivals*.

Having a worthy rival, someone who can help you to bring out the best in yourself, is a great advantage to anyone looking to maximise their performance potential.

Difficult moments in the market should be seen the same way as facing a difficult opponent in a sporting event. It could be something to fear and avoid – or it could be a worthy rival, an opportunity to test yourself, for development and for growth that will ultimately contribute towards becoming your best trading self.

"When a challenge confronts you, remember that God is matching
you with a younger sparring partner, as would a physical trainer.
Why? Becoming an Olympian takes sweat! I think no one has a better
challenge than yours, if only you would use it like an athlete would that
younger sparring partner."

– Epictetus

DEVELOPING A BULLETPROOF MINDSET

By shifting your mindset from seeing stress as harmful, to seeing stress as normal and helpful – by seeing losses, setbacks and challenges as opportunities to learn from, develop and refine your trading process – you can shift your experience of, and relationship with, challenge and difficulty in the markets.

Difficult experiences can be seen as worthy rivals, sent to help you improve and build towards mastery over the long term.

What beliefs about stress, difficulty and challenge – about risk, uncertainty, losing, mistakes, drawdowns – would be useful for you to hold as a trader?

6

TAKE COMMITTED ACTION

THE MOTIVATION TRAP

O VER THE YEARS I have been fortunate to work with thousands of new traders entering the markets for the first time, primarily as graduates at investment banks or on training programmes at proprietary trading groups. Almost every new trader I have worked with has told me that they are motivated, often *highly* motivated, to achieve success in trading. Most tell me that they are willing to do "whatever it takes".

Motivation is wanting to be successful. *Commitment*, however, is actually doing what is required to become successful.

Motivation is a feeling. It certainly mobilises energy for taking action, but it is transient – it comes and goes.

So what happens when our motivation is low, perhaps during a period of drawdown, or in quieter or more challenging markets? How will this impact taking effective trading action?

Consider these two questions.

1. For the rest of your trading career you only take the specific actions that are required to maximise your chances of success in trading if you are feeling motivated – you are in the mood, trading is going well, you are making money, you are psyched-up and feeling good.

2. For the rest of your trading career you take the specific actions that are required to maximise your chances of success in trading – whether you are motivated or not, in the mood or not, whether you feel good or bad, whether you are making money or losing money, optimistic or pessimistic, calm or anxious, relaxed or fearful, energetic or tired, confident or not.

Which would you choose?

Many people link taking specific action to being in a particular mindset, mood, or having a required level of motivation. In trading, however, it is often the case that action will need to be taken even when the desired internal experience is not present.

- Traders have to be able to take market opportunities that present themselves, even though difficult thoughts and emotions around losing may be showing up following a previous losing trade or a string of losses.

- Traders need to be able to stay in winning trades, even though thoughts and emotions around the potential for future regret may be showing up.

- Traders have to be able to take losses, even though difficult thoughts and emotions about taking the loss and the possibility of the 'market coming back' may be showing up.

It is commonplace for traders to *have* to take effective trading action while co-existing with difficult internal thoughts, emotions and physical sensations.

FROM MOTIVATION TO COMMITMENT

Commitment is about being action-focused. It is about taking action, doing what is needed, even when motivation is low, or you are tired, or you are feeling anxious. Or, in fact, when you are having any difficult internal experience.

Commitment is long lasting. It cuts through motivation. It doesn't require you to feel a particular way; it just requires you take effective action in that moment.

When you take action you create shifts in your mind and body. Taking action in itself can lead to increased feelings of motivation. Action can actually be antecedent to motivation.

Act first, then feel as a result.

Over the many years I have spent working with high performers across numerous high-performance domains, I have come to realise that while motivation is an important factor in achieving success, *commitment is far more significant.* It is by far the greater determinant of success. It is also one of the core factors of psychological flexibility and of stress hardiness and mental toughness.

COMMITTED ACTION

Suppose you wanted to be victorious at the Olympic Games. Epictetus says:

"That's fine, but fully consider what you're getting yourself into. What does such a desire entail? What needs to happen first? Then what? What will be required of you? And what else follows from that? Is this whole course of action really beneficial to you? If so, carry on. If you wish to win at the Olympic Games, to prepare yourself properly you would have to follow a strict regimen that stretches you to the limits of your endurance. You would have to submit to demanding rules, follow a suitable diet, vigorously exercise at a regular time in both heat and cold, and give up drinking. You would have to follow the directions of your trainer as if he or she were your doctor."[12]

Committed action is about regularly and consistently taking the steps that increase your chances of success in trading – that increase your edge. In their book *The Psychology of Enhancing Human Performance*, Gardner and Moore define commitment as being "demonstrated when one regularly and consistently demonstrates the specific behaviours and activities that are likely to directly result in optimal performance".[13]

In the short term this relates to the execution of your trading strategy, and what might commonly be referred to as *discipline* or *poise*.

In the longer term it is about sustaining effective action, through the highs and lows of trading, which could be termed *perseverance*.

Trading at your best and achieving your full trading potential requires you to be able to do both – to be disciplined and to persevere.

What are the specific behaviours and actions that you need to take that are likely to result in you trading at your best and achieving your full trading potential?

What specific actions will be most effective for you to take in the most challenging and difficult of situations – taking a loss, holding a winning trade, during a period of drawdown, after making a mistake?

COMMITTED ACTION IS UNCONDITIONAL

It is important to state that it is not possible to take conditional committed action.[14] You are committed, or not.

Here are some examples of how traders place conditions on their trading actions:

'Sure, I will take this loss just as long I don't have to feel bad about it.'

'I will stay in this trade just as long as I don't have to feel regret about what happens if I make the wrong decision.'

'I am happy to take bigger risk as long as I don't have to feel the anxiety of doing so.'

Committed action is full commitment, with no desire to feel better or good, and with no guarantee of success. Each trade you make requires this mindset. Each step you take in becoming a better trader also requires this approach.

The idea of full commitment with no guarantee of success, and with no attachment to the outcome, is something that I have worked on with many of my trading clients. It always plays a huge part in helping traders to reduce their stress and anxiety levels and to improve trading execution.

What difficult internal experiences (thoughts, emotions, sensations) that may show up as you take action towards achieving your trading goals are you willing to make room for?

POISE – THE ART OF DISCIPLINED TRADING

"The greatest cause of stress for me within trading is when I do not follow my trading plan, when I do not keep a certain trade within my risk parameters, when I do not follow my pre-determined rules for a trade. This can work me up and make me frustrated and that's when I turn to writing a few lines to myself and then making sure the very next trade I follow those rules which I have set myself again."

– An investment bank trader

In the short term, commitment and taking committed action is about executing your trading process consistently – it is about what we might in general terms refer to as discipline. Discipline is a core trading topic. When I ask my clients to explain what it means to them, it is often defined as *'having a plan and sticking to the plan'*. All traders can think of times when, under that definition, they have 'lost discipline' – when they knew what they wanted to do, but didn't do it.

Poise is the ability to take committed action, to execute your trading process, even in the presence of difficult thoughts, emotions and sensations. It is a myth that high performers in key moments like a football World Cup penalty shootout are stress- and anxiety-free. High performers and the best traders are performing *not in the absence of stress or pressure, but in its presence*. This is poise.

Being able to perform with poise has three key components:

- **Commitment** – knowing what matters, what action to take (your trading process) and being committed to doing it.

- **Awareness** – having awareness of your internal experience, the thoughts, emotions and sensations that are showing up; and external awareness, of the market environment.

- **Willingness** – being willing to accept the discomfort that may show up in your trading.

PERSEVERANCE – KEEPING GOING WHEN THE GOING GETS TOUGH

In your trading have you ever asked yourself 'Why am I doing this?' If so, what had happened? What was the situation? Can you remember what your response was?

I have heard this question many times from traders when times have been particularly tough. Often my response is 'Why *are* you doing this?'

When times are difficult it is not unusual to question why you are doing what you are doing. It is a question that seeks to find a purpose, a reason for persevering, and an energy to tap into to keep moving forward.

As a bulletproof trader what is needed is a clear response to that question. And you have to know that answer *before* you find yourself asking it in the middle of a tough time.

Having a sense of your purpose, of why you trade, is a key ingredient in being bulletproof, and plays a big part in your ability to persevere when times are tough. Being able to tap into it can bring extra energy, focus and engagement when you need it most.

In tough times it is also useful to be able to lean on your values, to know the strengths and qualities of action that you want to bring this time.

How do you want to *be* in a period of difficulty?

Ultimately perseverance is a function of taking consistent committed action over time. It means doing what needs to be done over and over again, so as to overcome the challenges and difficulties of trading. It involves adapting your trading style and behaviour to changing markets, working through periods of drawdown, bouncing back from losses, and keeping moving forward – all to maximise the chances of trading success.

> "The cucumber is bitter? Then throw it out. There are brambles in the path? Then go around. That's all you need to know."
>
> **– Marcus Aurelius**

STRENGTHENING COMMITMENT

The stronger your commitment, the greater your discipline (poise) – and your perseverance.

To become bulletproof, I encourage traders to actively strengthen their commitment by:

1. *Knowing your purpose* – why you are trading and what you want from your trading. (**Why?**)

2. *Knowing your values* – who you want to be as a trader, the character strengths and qualities of action you want to cultivate, and how this links to your purpose. (**Who?**)

3. *Knowing your process* – be clear about the specific steps you need to take to maximise your chances of success, and how these link to your purpose, values and goals. (**How?**)

7

KNOW YOUR VALUES

A DIFFERENT APPROACH

I AM SITTING IN a large hotel conference room on a Monday morning listening to the CEO of a successful global trading business deliver a speech. He's kicking off the start of a week-long off-site retreat involving the company's senior leaders, trading managers and top trading and research talent.

The speech has stuck in my mind ever since. It was so different to the speeches I normally hear at this type of event:

> "I want our focus this year to be on professionalism – on being the best professionals we can be in our respective roles. I want everyone to think about what that means for them. How will you act and behave in yourself and towards others as a result? With the talent we have within this business, I believe that if we all commit to being the best professionals we can, to doing our roles as well as we possibly can, we will get the best performance we can. The market and other external factors will determine what that means for our P&L."

What struck me about this speech is that it did not start with a number. Or a result. Or an outcome that had to be achieved and then a focus on how that could be achieved through a particular strategy. It started with a way of being.

It began with a quality of action, which would drive specific behaviours.

It acknowledged uncontrollable factors and their impact on what would happen. It didn't deny them or pretend they could necessarily be overcome. It focused on what could be controlled. And at the heart of that was values.

It was, in other words, *a values-based approach to performance.*

Typical approach to performance

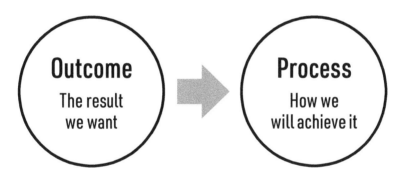

Values-based approach to performance

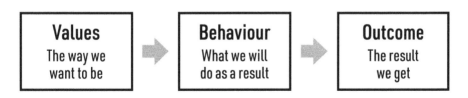

THE VALUE OF VALUES

We've established the importance of commitment and how taking committed action in the short term (discipline/poise) and in the longer term (perseverance) are important. But how do we achieve them? To help traders strengthen their commitment and perseverance, I bring a more conscious focus to their values.

Being clear about your values – what matters most to you – is powerful in all high-performance pursuits.

When I work with traders, I spend time helping them elicit and then clarify what those values really are. We look at what matters most to them personally and what is important in their trading. We cover the character strengths and qualities of actions they want to cultivate.

For anyone working in a corporate environment, the mention of the word 'values' can evoke a groan. I understand that. In many institutions, mission statements and lists of values are put out merely because it is expected. Often they are dramatically disconnected from the experience of employees or other stakeholders on the ground. I witnessed this for myself when working with a trading institution which had a wonderful set of values – with some fantastic posters on the walls to illustrate them – but in talking with the trading and management teams there was a real dissonance between those values and visible behaviours.

In order to avoid the abstract I prefer to think instead of values as *chosen qualities of action*; as behavioural strengths and characteristics. Things that you can practise, ways of being.

Underlying our values are verbally constructed rules that motivate us to act in ways that are meaningful to us.[15] When you trade in accordance with your values you will be guided to taking effective action, even when difficult internal experiences show up.

In the absence of values people tend to be motivated by being right, looking good in the eyes of others, avoiding difficult internal events and doing what is good in the short term – even if doing so is not in their long-term interests.[16]

UNCOVERING YOUR VALUES

Take time to think about your answers to these questions – write them down somewhere:

- How do you want to be as a trader?
- What strengths and qualities of action do you want to demonstrate in your trading?
- Think of a role model that you have – in trading or outside of trading. What are the strengths and qualities that you most admire in them?

Make a list of your responses and reflect on them.

Once you have a list of your valued strengths and qualities of action, a good next step is to make a hierarchy of the top five.

BUILDING PATTERNS OF VALUES-BASED COMMITTED ACTION

One of the real benefits of spending some time defining your trading values is that you can utilise them to *build patterns of committed action*. Actions that are underpinned by values are far more robust under stress and adversity than actions that are not. They are deep intrinsic motivators and drivers of behaviour.

Turning values into actions is an important and oft-missed step. The basic process is to think about what specific actions you can take in your trading that reflect your values. You are deriving your actions from your values. You can also link your values to your goals, strengthening your commitment to them, and then think about what actions will help you to achieve your goals and are aligned with your values. This is a powerful way to build committed action, poise and perseverance.

For each of your top five trading values think about three specific behaviours that would reflect that value in your trading.

Turning values into actions

Value	Trading behaviours

VALUES, STRESS AND DIFFICULTY

Researchers at Stanford University analysed 15 years of studies involving people's values and found that when people connected to their values they were:

- more likely to believe that they could change difficult situations

- more likely to take positive action instead of seeking avoidance

- more likely to see their adverse situation as temporary.[17]

Over time this mindset of taking positive action builds upon itself, shifting the narratives that people tell themselves when they are stressed and having a tough time, encouraging further positive action to be taken and reinforcing beliefs that subsequently enable them to see themselves as able to cope with adversity.

This creates what the researchers termed a "narrative of personal adequacy".

In a study conducted at Stanford, students were asked to keep a journal over the winter holidays.[18] One group of students was asked to write about their values and how the day's activities reflected those values. A second group was asked to write about three good things that happened to them that day. Following the winter break the journals were collected and analysed. The group that had written about their values had better health and felt more confident in their abilities to handle stress at college. Interestingly, *the most positive impact on writing about their values was had by those who had experienced the greatest stress over the holiday period.*

Writing about your values has been shown to be a highly effective psychological intervention, with short-term benefits including feeling more in control and mentally strong, increased pain tolerance, increased self-control and reduced rumination after difficult experiences. And, in the longer term, improved health and wellbeing. Even just one ten-minute period of writing about your values demonstrated benefits in the future.

Pick one of your top five trading values and write about it for ten minutes.

Describe why this value is important to you. How do you express this value in your trading? (Including what you did today.)

Write about how this value might guide you when facing a difficult time or decision in your trading.

ARETE

A key part of the Stoic's philosophy was the principle of living with *arete*, meaning virtue or excellence. It's about expressing your best self in *every* moment, being the best version of yourself in the here and now. Acting in line with deep values.

I was once contacted by a sports trader seeking advice for dealing with adverse situations within his trading. One of the bits of guidance I gave him that resonated was the idea of connecting with your valued strengths and behaviours when times are tough; thinking about what you want to stand for, how you want to be.

When faced with a challenging or difficult moment in your trading, asking yourself these questions can help you bring to mind values, strengths and qualities that enable you to take effective action.

'How can I bring my best trading self to this moment or situation?'

'Who do I want to *be* in this moment or time of difficulty?'

Think about some of the challenging and difficult situations that you face in your own trading.

- What value would be useful to bring to mind, to guide your response in each situation?

- What would be the effective values-based behaviour it would drive?

Situation	Value	Values-based effective action

Having a connection to your valued character strengths and qualities of action makes you better able to bring the best trading version of yourself to stressful moments and difficult times in the markets – and navigate them successfully.

"First say to yourself what you would be; and then do what you would have to do."

– Epictetus

PART FOUR

RISK AND UNCERTAINTY

8

MANAGE YOUR RISK

RISK, STRESS AND TRADING DECISIONS

T HE HUMAN BRAIN is optimised for assessing threats and risks. Within the brain lie circuits and mechanisms honed to constantly monitor for risk and reward, threat and opportunity.

This basic monitoring system is core to your survival. Firstly, you must stay alive by not getting killed (risk). Then, while you are alive, you must seek to *stay* alive and maintain the population, primarily through eating and reproducing (reward). The latter only matters, of course, if you achieve the former, so threat assessment and risk management are highly developed and deeply seated processes within the brain.

When you enter a position into the market you are taking a risk. In doing so you will be engaging your risk-detection process. Firstly you'll be assessing: 'Is this a threat?' If yes, then: 'How dangerous is this threat?' And finally, 'Do I have the resources to cope with this threat?'

If you have the psychological, physiological and financial resources to cope with the risk that you have taken, your body will enter into a *challenge response*, a performance-enhancing state.[19] If the risk you have taken is in excess of your psychological, physiological and financial resources, your body will enter a *threat response*. This is a performance-debilitating state, resulting in reduced cognitive capabilities, including decision-making and self-control.

> "Trading is very stressful for me when I have too big a position on in a market that looks like it could go thin or extra volatile or I've a relatively large position and am heavily offside. This can distract me from other opportunities as I'm so focused on the position that's concerning me. I'd also say that when I have a big position on (bigger than I'm comfortable with) it affects my trade management – I may not hold the trade to target as the P&L swings are too enticing to hold, or I may not stop out at the price I say I will because I don't want to realise the loss."
>
> **– A hedge fund trader**

The amount of risk that you take in the market will impact how much stress you subject yourself to, and the amount of stress that you subject yourself to will have an impact on your trading decisions. The goal is to find ways of optimising your risk-taking so that you can balance executing your trading strategy as effectively as possible with maximising the opportunities the market presents you – and your overall market returns.

THE ART OF OPTIMAL RISK-TAKING

"The most stressful situations for me tend to arise when I am trading either too much size or too many products at one time. I tend to lose composure somewhat in these situations and make hasty decisions that in hindsight are rarely the right decisions but more or less taken so as to relieve stress in the immediate short term. This leads to frustration in the long term."

– A futures trader

I have come across traders who experienced significant stress over their trading, at the core of which was taking positions they were not psychologically, physiologically or financially prepared for – especially when the positions moved against them.

Sometimes the pressure to make P&L leads to traders taking risk well outside their comfort zone, leading to a reduction in decision-making quality – and further losses. It can become a vicious cycle. Of course, when traders take excessive risk and win it feels great – but while there is a short increase in pleasure, at a discipline and process level the likelihood of success in the long term if this behaviour is repeated is reduced.

From a bulletproof perspective, the goal is *optimal risk-taking*. That means finding your own balance: trading positions as big as is right for you and your strategy in any given trading opportunity, while still being able to execute your trading process effectively.

As Steve Clark puts it in *Hedge Fund Market Wizards*: "Trade within your emotional capacity".[20] Or, as Joe Vidich puts it, "Limit your size in any position so that fear does not become the prevailing instinct guiding your judgement."[21]

I once delivered a day of training for the top trading talent of a major investment bank. At the dinner that concluded the event, the global head of trading, a well-respected and successful trader, gave a short speech. And in that speech he talked about the "sweet spot" of risk-taking – and how crucially important it was to find *a balance between opportunity maximisation and disciplined execution*. He also talked memorably about the dangers and problems that arise from exceeding the sweet spot – from getting caught up in excessive risk-taking.

THE RISK SWEET SPOT

If we plot risk and performance on a curve we can see that there is an inverted-U relationship between the two. When risk is too low, performance is also low. At this point traders are likely to be trading so small that they do not pay full attention to their positions. They may let them run further against them than usual. They get complacent and bored. Decision-making and trading process are often not well executed here.

At the far end, when too much risk is taken, the threat response activates: emotions run high, stress levels are high, worry and fear show up. Decision-making and trading process are often not well executed here either.

In the middle, though, is that sweet spot: the zone of optimal risk-taking – where profit-maximisation and strategy execution are in balance.

How do you find it?

For many traders it happens through trial and error. For some, research and modelling. One simple test is that if you are experiencing high levels of anxiety, stress and fear in your positions, you may simply be trading too big for that particular context.

Risk and performance – the zone of optimal risk-taking

Assessing position size has to be done in context – this curve is individual to each trader, and to each market and strategy that a trader trades, as well as to other contextual factors such as overall market exposure, current P&L and financial capital.

Many factors will affect where the position-size optimal zone will be, including:

- experience and skill level
- individual risk tolerance
- strategy
- market liquidity and volatility
- current P&L
- physiological state
- level of market risk/event risk
- how many positions a trader has on.

Because markets are dynamic, these contexts are always shifting – so position sizing and risk management will be a dynamic process. I have seen traders make the mistake of getting locked into trading positions of a fixed size, irrespective of market conditions and their own psychological and physiological state.

I often use the metaphor of windsurfing to illustrate the importance of being flexible in position sizing. Windsurfers pick a combination of board and sail that helps them maximise their performance in the context of the type of sailing they want to do, e.g. speed, slalom, race, wave sailing, freestyle etc., and the weather and water conditions.

Taking out a large board and huge sail in very windy weather will not be a particularly enjoyable or successful experience. (Even if your ego enjoys having the biggest sail on the water.)

Professional windsurfers are focused on selecting the board and sail combination that allows them to perform at their best, not which looks the best or satisfies ego. Traders need to do this for position sizing.

Be mindful of the market conditions, your strategy, your own state and any other important factors – and then choose the size and strategy combination that maximises opportunity while allowing you to maintain quality execution of your plan.

RISK-AWARE DECISION-MAKING

Risk-aware decision-making is about bringing a greater awareness to the risk you take in your trading. It means being mindful of the internal and external contexts that influence your risk-taking. It's a dynamic process and requires flexibility. There is a great example of being flexible with positioning in *Hedge Fund Market Wizards*:

"Martin Taylor (Nevsky Capital) came into 2008 with a large net long exposure in high beta stocks in an increasingly risky market. Uncomfortable with the level of his exposure, Taylor sharply reduced his positions in early January. When the market subsequently plunged later in the month, he was well positioned to increase his long exposure. Had Taylor remained heavily net long, he might have instead been forced to sell into the market weakness to reduce risk, thereby missing out in fully participating in the subsequent rebound."[22]

It is not about how big your positions are. It is about balancing opportunity maximisation with execution and decision quality, about reducing excessive stress exposure, and maximising your market returns.

9

EMBRACE UNCERTAINTY

WHICH BOX?

THERE ARE TWO closed boxes in front of you. Box A has 100 balls in it. Fifty are red and 50 are blue. Box B has 100 balls in it. They are red and blue, but you do not know how many are red and how many are blue.

Your task, in order to win a prize is, is to select a colour ball and the box from which you intend to pick it.

Which colour ball would you aim for? Which box would you choose?

The choice of ball colour is not of any real interest to us here, but the choice of box definitely is. Which box do you think most people choose from? If you said box A, you would be correct.

Why is box A more popular than B?

It's all about certainty. The known.

It is entirely possible that the chances of selecting your colour ball are significantly higher in box B, but the odds are *unknown*. Of course, the chances could also be much worse. There is a lack of certainty. The comfort that comes with the known – or perhaps the discomfort of the unknown – drives people towards A.

This is interesting from a trading perspective because trading the markets is experientially much more like choosing from box B than choosing from A – there is uncertainty, unknowns; risks that cannot be calculated with complete accuracy.

MARKETS, TRADERS AND UNCERTAINTY

It is a part of the human condition that people have a general preference for certainty over uncertainty. However, the markets are not stable or certain. As Mark Douglas put it: "Every moment in the market is unique".[23]

We do not know for certain what is going to happen next. This can bring feelings of anxiety as future potential market scenarios run through your mind and all the potential consequences are played out. One of the key challenges that traders therefore face is developing the ability to manage the uncertainty of the markets.

Imagine you are sat at a computer screen in a lab playing a game. The game involves you selecting certain rocks on your screen – but with a catch. Snakes are hidden behind some of the rocks. If you choose one of them you are given a slightly painful shock to your hand. As you are playing, the computer estimates your level of uncertainty for each choice you are making and simultaneously measures your stress levels by monitoring your pupil dilation and perspiration.

This was actually a real study carried out at University College London.[24] The results showed that people were most stressed when they were most uncertain. In fact, it was more stressful being highly uncertain about finding a snake than being certain you *would* find a snake.

Uncertainty, and particularly uncertainty about potential bad outcomes, is stressful – and traders are exposed to this on a frequent basis.

How often does everything in your trading work out exactly to plan? Probably very rarely. The markets are dynamic and uncertain. You cannot change the nature of the markets, but you *can* change how you respond to them.

You can develop a mental framework and skills that allow you to manage the uncertainty of the markets more effectively.

IMPERMANENCE

"No man ever steps into the same river twice, for it's not the same river, and he is not the same man."

– Heraclitus

Impermanence is a principle I picked up from my training in mindfulness. It's also a key part of Stoic philosophy. It relates to the idea that everything is in a constant state of change, from moment to moment and over time. Internally, your thoughts, emotions and sensations are forever shifting. Externally, so are the markets.

Adopting a mindset of impermanence means, in essence, *accepting* the uncertainty of both your internal and external experiences. This can help to reduce stress and anxiety. Integrating impermanence into your mental framework also offers the ability to become more flexible in your trading behaviour – being open to the shifts and changes in market dynamics, and being able to flex your trading style and strategy accordingly.

The mindset of impermanence plays a significant role in the experience of losing runs, drawdown periods and tough times. It reminds you that a losing run is impermanent. It is not forever. Periods of change in the market are also impermanent. They are not forever. And changes in your P&L are impermanent. *They* are not forever.

Nothing stays the same forever in trading or in life; both are impermanent.

PRACTISING UNCERTAINTY

Getting good at dealing with uncertainty happens when you are exposed to uncertainty. Being exposed to uncertainty, and learning how be with it and navigate through it, is the best thing we can do.

One of the ways I help my clients to develop their appreciation of impermanence, and the constant shifting and changing of the inner and outer worlds, is through a mindfulness-based mental training technique known as *open-awareness training*. I have provided a brief outline of this practice below.

This open awareness mindfulness-based mental training practice will help you to develop your experience of experiencing – and becoming more comfortable with – uncertainty and the impermanence of our experience.

Get into a comfortable seated position, feet flat on the floor, back straight, upright, but relaxed.

Relax your shoulders, neck and arms as much as you can. Take time to release any tension you may feel. Take a deep breath and relax as you breathe out.

Close your eyes if you like. If you would prefer to keep them open, look down at the floor in front of you with a relaxed gaze.

For a few moments focus your full attention toward your breathing... allow your mind to settle and stabilise on the breath... breathing in, breathing out...

Now... let go of the attention on your breathing and open up to whatever may arise.

When the first distraction attracts your attention... a sound... a thought... a physical sensation... or anything else... direct your full attention to it and use it to anchor your awareness.

Observe the distraction neutrally, like watching your breath, like observing waves at the beach. Don't think about it... don't engage it... don't try to make it stay or go away. Just observe it.

If it feels difficult to have a neutral approach to the distraction – if you notice you start to engage with it – it can be helpful to give it a short mental label. If a thought arises about the markets, you could label it 'markets' and observe the experience of the thought without thinking about the content of the thought. Or you could use even simpler labels such as 'thought', 'sound', 'feeling'.

Notice when a distraction comes into focus... notice it is there... notice when at some point it changes into something else or disappears.

When a distraction disappears, open up and be ready to receive the next one the same way.

If at any time you become overwhelmed or you need to stabilise your attention, pause... relax... release the distractions and return your focus fully to your breath. After a while, when you have stabilised your focus again, let go of your breathing and open up your awareness again

At any time you can always come back to the anchor and simply focus on your breath.

THIS IS WHAT HAPPENS IN THE BATHHOUSE

Stoic philosopher Epictetus tells us that if we go to the bathhouse then it is likely that we will find people there who "jostle, splash and even steal", and that we can either get upset about that, or we can remind ourselves that *this is what happens in the bathhouse.*

If we do the latter, then we are less likely to get upset or annoyed by what happens because we understand that this is simply an inherent part of that environment.[25]

One of the interesting paradoxes of traders and the challenge of uncertainty is that when I speak with clients about why they got into trading, or what they enjoy about trading, very frequently the word *variety* comes up. They have chosen to trade because they enjoy the variety. The less predictable nature of the work. Yet this variety is essentially driven by the uncertainty and novelty of trading – they are two sides of the same piece of paper.

Would you swap uncertainty for certainty? Would you swap variety for boredom?

In trading, markets move unexpectedly, novel events happen, data is not always as expected. Trump tweets, micro-crashes occur, things do not always move as you expect them to move. If you accept that all of these events and situations can happen, that they are a feature of trading the markets, a part of the environment, then you will be less disturbed by them.

Everything that is about to come is uncertain, so embrace it. You have no control over what the market will do in the future, only how you will respond to those events.

10

PLAN FOR THE WORST

PREPARE FOR SUCCESS

PEOPLE PERFORMING IN high-stakes, high-pressure environments such as elite athletes and sports teams, the military, and top traders and fund managers, have long recognised the importance of being well prepared in order to perform at their best.

Preparation and planning is the first stage of the high-performance cycle and influences how well you execute and manage your trades.

The high-performance cycle

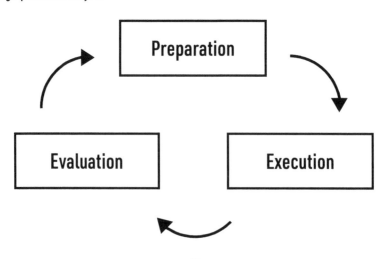

There are several key benefits to being well prepared for trading the markets, including:

- **Consistency** – repeating your preparation process gives you an opportunity to establish a sense of consistency within your trading process.

- **Confidence** – knowing that you have not prepared fully gives you an uneasy feeling; it can create doubt and conflict, reduce your confidence and impact your execution.

- **Control** – how well you prepare for the market is largely under your control – it is one of the few trading variables that you have high levels of control over.

- **Composure** – if you are well prepared, and especially if you have conducted some scenario planning and 'if-then' processes, then it can enable you to stay more composed and act more effectively in challenging market moments.

- **Concentration** – your preparation routine can become a 'trigger' that engages your mind on your trading, helping you to transition from one mindset to another, e.g. from waking and getting to the screens to a trading mindset.

Confidence, control, composure and concentration are all valuable mental assets to take with you into trading the markets, and all play a key part in being bulletproof.

Of course, how individual traders prepare will vary from person to person – influenced by the markets they trade, their trading strategies and their own preferences. Generally, I find that most traders conduct some form of preparation that covers analysis of news, data, fundamentals and technical, and the identification of possible trading opportunities. The preparation is often biased towards what I would call the 'technical/tactical' and does not always cover the 'mental/emotional', which is important in developing greater levels of bulletproofing to adverse events in the markets.

WHAT IF?

"Being unexpected adds to the weight of a disaster, and being a surprise has never failed to increase a person's pain. For that reason, nothing should ever be unexpected by us. Our minds should be sent out to all things and we shouldn't just consider the normal course of things, but what could actually happen. For is there anything in life that Fortune won't knock off its high horse if it pleases her?"

– Seneca

Imagine being at the Olympic Games. It is the day of your event, your time to perform at potentially the pinnacle of your sporting career. You have spent most of your athletic life training to get here. Over the last four-year Olympic cycle you've been 100% committed to your training. All for this moment.

You feel in the best shape of your life. And, although you are experiencing some nerves about the event, you cannot wait to get there and get started on your warm-up routine and into competitive mode.

Now imagine you get to the bus stop at the athlete village and the bus does not arrive. There is a problem. It turns up late. You won't have time to warm-up as you practised.

Or, imagine you are an open water swimmer or triathlete who at the start of the race has their goggles kicked off.

How would you feel? What would you do?

Many unplanned situations arise at major sporting events. When these events occur they throw an athlete off their game – unless they have trained and prepared for them. Over the years, one of the most important elements that sports psychologists have added to their repertoire of strategies when working with athletes is to look at a range of different scenarios that could potentially occur – and to equip their clients with the technical and psychological skills to deal with them effectively. Including training for them and rehearsing them in advance.

This process is often referred to as 'what-if', or 'if-then', planning. It is something I advocate for all my trading clients.

IF-THEN

'What-if' scenario planning is an important and effective strategy to add to your trading preparation if you are not already doing so. One of its most useful benefits is that it helps to reduce the stress and anxiety that can come from uncertainty by considering what uncertain events may happen in advance. It also helps in developing strategies for dealing with them.

This is what I refer to as *planned uncertainty*.

> "The most stressful trading situations for me have been big major risk events like Brexit and big European elections etc. Mainly due to the increased volatility. To deal with these situations I try to plan well in advance, starting with creating what-if statements and researching them among a group of traders, e.g. 'What if Trump gets impeached? What will that do to the markets I trade? And what scenarios can I look at for possible examples?'"
>
> **– A hedge fund trader**

'What-if' scenario planning is, in my experience, always more effective when conducted not just as a process of listing scenarios you believe are possible, but when combined with a very definite focus on 'here is how I will respond in that situation'. (This makes it more of an 'if-then' process.)

'If-then' planning can help you to feel more confident. You know that you are ready to deal with any upcoming challenges. You are also more composed if they *do* happen, as they have already been identified.

Planned uncertainty like this gives you a small dose of exposure to the potential stressor, which reduces your future stress response – and with a plan of action already in place you are better able to respond strategically rather than react emotionally.

THE PRE-MORTEM

The Stoics were great fans of planning for the worst. Anticipating what might go wrong on journeys, with decisions, or in life in general, was a key part of their philosophy. "*Nothing happens to the wise man against his expectation, nor do all things turn out for him as he wished but as he reckoned – and above all he reckoned that something could block his plans.*" wrote Seneca.

They were ready for difficulty, setbacks and disruption. And not only did they focus on anticipating such events, but also on how they would deal with them. The Stoics were strong believers in controlling what is controllable and recognising, and not attempting to control, that which is not.

They recognised that many things could interfere with even the best-made plans, so they prepared for the worst. This practice of planning for the worst was known as *premeditation malorum* (premeditation of evils).[26]

Most people are familiar with a post-mortem analysis – the idea of analysing an event or a decision after the outcome is known. Many traders do a post-mortem analysis of their trading decisions. *But what about a pre-mortem?*

The pre-mortem is a process popularised by psychologist Gary Klein. It is a valuable tool for enhancing decision-making. Rather than looking forward from the present to assess what *might* happen, it takes an imagined future perspective on what *has* happened – a technique known as 'prospective hindsight'.[27]

Imagine you are a part of a research study and you are asked the question: *'How likely is it that a woman will be elected the leader of your country in the first election after the next one?'* Think about all the reasons why this might happen. For specificity, provide a numerical probability.

Now consider another version of the question, using prospective hindsight: 'Imagine that the first election after the next one *has* occurred and a woman has been elected the leader of your country.' Think about all the reasons why this might have happened. Again, provide a numerical probability of this actually occurring.

Research shows that the second question, taking a future perspective – utilising prospective hindsight 'as if it had happened' – generated a greater number of ideas (25% more in one study), and higher predicted probability of the event actually occurring.[28]

A trading pre-mortem involves taking yourself into the future and imagining that your trade has not worked out in some way. Then, from that future perspective, thinking about all the reasons why it did not work out – and, ideally, documenting them. You can then take these insights to make any adjustments needed to the trade plan *before* you execute it.

TRADING PRE-MORTEM

Before making your trade:

- Imagine being in the future at a point where your trade has failed – lost.

- From that 'in the future perspective' think about all of the reasons it could have happened. Write them down.

Bring these insights back to the present and utilise them in your trading planning.

This type of process is sometimes referred to as negative visualisation. By thinking about the obstacles and difficulties that might happen, and how you might respond to them, we develop emotional resilience – and train ourselves to maintain a greater level of equanimity in challenging situations.

One client I worked with who utilised the pre-mortem effectively was a fund manager from a major asset manager. He had become concerned that he was missing out on opportunities in the market and was losing P&L as a result. We implemented the pre-mortem by getting him to spend the start of the day taking himself into the future – to the end of the day – and imagining he had missed out on some opportunities. Then he would assess the reasons this had happened. He would write down those insights and bring them back to the present – and take any useful ones and implement them in his trade plans and portfolio-construction ideas.

PART
FIVE

FOCUS

11

TRAIN YOUR ATTENTION

ATTENTION MATTERS

I N HIS BOOK, *The Attention Revolution*, B. Alan Wallace states that: "Few things affect our lives more than the faculty of attention. If we can't focus our attention – we can't do anything well."[29] Being able to focus, to pay attention to what matters, is a key performance skill – whether you are a trader, athlete, musician, surgeon or pilot, or performing in any kind of way.

Where you place your attention influences your thoughts, emotions, feelings and behaviours. It impacts on the brain. Neural pathways are used, formed and strengthened as a result.

Where your attention goes, your energy flows.

In trading, the quality of your attention determines:

- your ability to focus on executing the specific steps of your trading process

- you attentiveness to market cues and information

- your ability to sustain that attention over extended periods of time

- your ability to recognise when you have become distracted – perhaps by market noise or by your own inner noise – and then refocus

- your level of self-awareness, particularly your *in-the-moment awareness*

- your ability to self-monitor and self-regulate your thoughts, emotions and body sensations.

Your attentional capacity contributes to your overall mental or cognitive fitness, and can provide important neurological benefits that increase a trader's level of resilience, reduce stress reactivity, enhance emotional regulation, reduce impulsivity and improve overall health and wellbeing.

A well-developed attentional capacity is, then, a key attribute of bulletproof trading.

TRAINING ATTENTION

Attention is a trainable skill. Focused attention can be developed through practices that encourage you to pay attention to the internal (thoughts, feelings, sensations) or external (sounds, sights, smells) as they are encountered.

Focused attention training improves your attentional abilities by increasing:

- the ability to direct your attention to what matters

- the ability to sustain your attention for longer

- the ability to notice more quickly when you have become distracted

- the ability to refocus more quickly.

A typical *focused-attention practice* might utilise your breathing as the object of attention. It would see you focus your entire attention on your incoming and outgoing breath. You have to try to sustain your attention there without distraction. If you get distracted, you then calmly return your attention to the breath and start again.

Using your breath as the focal point has several advantages, including portability and the opportunity to practise anywhere. The breath also only ever occurs in the present moment – providing an anchor point to the present. And it gives access to your body's physical sensations.

One fund manager I worked with who spent time training his attention noted: "Since practising the focused attention training exercises I have really noticed that I have become far more attentive, and less distracted, both in and out of trading." Research by Mark Fenton-O'Creevy using mindfulness-based focused attention training practices with traders found that "[e]ven brief interventions can successfully induce a mindful state, improve attention, increase capacity to monitor financial information, and improve financial decision-making".[30]

FOCUSED ATTENTION TRAINING PRACTICE

In this focused attention training practice you are going to use your breath as the focus of your attention. The aim is to sit comfortably and then simply allow your attention to settle on the sensations of your breathing, following the rhythm and speed of your breath, the movements of your chest and abdomen, feeling the flow of air in and out, just noticing. When your mind wanders simply notice where it went and then gently bring your attention back to the breath.

Start by sitting comfortably in an upright position. Close your eyes if you feel comfortable doing so, otherwise maintain a loose gaze towards the floor.

Focus your attention on one of your more prominent sensations of breathing – it could be the speed or rhythm, the feeling of your chest or diaphragm rising and falling, or the flow of air around the nostrils.

When you notice that your attention has drifted, and it will – usually quite quickly – bring it back to the sensations of breathing.

These attentional shifts – mind wandering – are normal; it is what minds do.

Recognising that the mind has wandered is a part of mindfulness training. No matter how many times your mind wanders, simply bring it back to the breath.

This practice can be completed over different time frames depending on the outcome you are after:

- 6–10 breaths for a quick focusing/re-focusing practice during the trading day.

- 3–5 minutes for those who are short of time, or who want a short formal practice, perhaps one to three times per day.

- 8–12 minutes for those wanting to maximise gains in minimal time – a daily practice.

- 15–20 minutes+, for those committed to a deeper practice and subsequent benefits.

ATTENTION-TRAINING BUILDS PRESENT-MOMENT AWARENESS

The process of paying attention to your experience in the present moment builds awareness – specifically, *present-moment awareness*. Awareness has two dimensions: firstly, noticing what you are thinking, feeling and doing, an internal awareness; secondly, an external awareness, the ability to be aware of what is going on around you, to be able to assess and absorb information from the external environment effectively and respond to it appropriately.

Self-awareness is a key high performance and bulletproof skill. Dr Travis Bradberry[31] conducted research across a range of different occupations and found that 83% of people who scored high for self-awareness were classified as high performers, and that just 2% of the lowest performers scored high on self-awareness.

Achieving very high levels of performance is dependent on being able to self-manage or self-regulate, and that is very much dependent on your self-awareness. You cannot manage your emotions, for example, if you are not aware of them. Bringing awareness to your thoughts, emotions and sensations in the moment, in real time, is the precursor to being able to regulate them – and is the basic neurological foundation of self-control, or trading discipline.

I often use the metaphor of being in a river to explain the benefits of developing present moment self-awareness. When you are in the river you are in the flow of the river; you go where it takes you. You experience the river in its different states, calm to rough, from *within* the water, and with little control – especially when you are in fast-flowing water or rapids. The ability to be aware of yourself, and to observe yourself, enables you to essentially be above the river instead – with a kind of helicopter view, noticing the conditions of the river from a very different perspective. The river is the same; your experience of it is different. And the choices that you can make are very different. It is this ability to notice, and then to be able to make effective choices, that is a key benefit to being more self-aware.

RESPONDING VS REACTING

"Then remind yourself that past and future have no power over you. Only the present – and even that can be minimized. Just mark off its limits."

– Marcus Aurelius

Developing your attention and your awareness provides a greater possibility of freedom and choice. It means enhanced control over your behaviour. You can become better able to respond to situations as you wish, rather than reacting automatically in the mental and emotional ruts of the past.

This ability to be responsive versus reactive is key for traders, especially when experiencing stressful moments or difficult times. The neuro-mechanics of the process are explained eloquently by Daniel Siegel of the Mindful Awareness Research Center UCLA in David Rock's book *Your Brain At Work*:

> "It's our ability to pause before we react… it gives us the space of mind in which we can consider various options and then choose the most appropriate ones… with the acquisition of a stabilised and refined focus on the mind itself, previously undifferentiated pathways of firing become detectable and then accessible to modification, it is in this way that we can use the mind to change the function and ultimately the structure of the brain."[32]

This ability to pause before we react is key to self-regulation and self-control, or as we might call it in trading terms – discipline.

Dr Kevin Ochsner, Head of the Social Cognitive Neuroscience Laboratory, Columbia University, explains self-awareness like this: "Self-awareness is the capacity to step outside your own skin and look at yourself with as close to an objective eye as is possible."[33] This ability to step outside yourself, to observe your own experience, has been likened by neuroscientists to having an impartial spectator, or an *observer self*.

THE OBSERVER

The present-moment awareness developed through focused-attention practice is, for me, the gold standard of self-awareness. It is training what we might refer to as your observer self. This is the part of you that notices, for example, what the other part of you is thinking or feeling. The part of you that is able to notice and be aware of any experience you are having.

One commodities trader who completed a course with me on trading using focused-attention training approaches was able to identify a key shift in his perspective: "When I am trading it is like I am watching from outside myself, a third-person perspective."

Former fund manager Tom Basso provides an interesting insight into his own self-awareness in Van K. Tharp's book *Super Trader*.

> "In situations where I felt I needed improvement or in which I wanted to improve my interactions with other people, I would just play key events back in my head – figuring out how others had handled the situation… I've always thought of it as some Tom Basso up in the corner of the room watching Tom Basso here talking to you in the room. The funny thing about this secondary observer was that as time went on, I found the observer showing up a lot more. It wasn't just at the end of the day anymore.

"As I got into stressful situations, as I started trading, doing more interacting with a lot of people, getting our business off the ground, dealing with clients, and so on. I found that this observer was there to help me through it. If I felt awkward or uneasy, then I was able to watch myself do it. Now I have this observer there all the time."[34]

Being able to objectively monitor and reflect on your own trading experience enables you to moderate and direct your behaviour. Self-awareness enables you to step outside the automatic flow of experience that we all encounter, and to access choice and flexibility over where you direct your attention and energy; to regulate your thoughts, feelings and behaviours.

THE OBSERVER SELF PRACTICE

Take a moment to sit comfortably and then take a couple of moments to do each of the following:

- Notice the points of contact between your body and what you are sitting on, and the floor.

- Notice any sounds around you.

- Notice your breath; the in-breath and the out-breath.

- Notice your thoughts.

- Notice how you are feeling.

And notice that there was a part of you that was listening to the sounds, doing the breathing, doing the thinking, having the feeling. And there was a part of you that was doing the noticing – the observer self.

12

FOCUS ON THE PROCESS

BEST DECISION VS WORST DECISION

Think about the *best* trading decision you have made over the last 12 months. Then think about the *worst* trading decision.

Now think about the outcome of each.

- Was the outcome of your good decision a win?
- Was the outcome of your bad trade a loss?

F YOU ARE like 99% of traders who I pose this question to in workshops, your answers will be *yes* and *yes*. It highlights how we have a tendency to judge the quality of our decisions based on the outcomes that we get from them. We have an *outcome bias*.

OUR OBSESSION WITH RESULTS

In trading, the outcome of a trade is of course important. Many traders and trading institutions obsess about it. Which is perfectly understandable. It is linked to compensation, status and career management. It is also objective and easy to measure and compare.

However, it may not be helpful for making your best trading decisions. Research into the impact of results-focused decision-making has found several downsides to becoming too outcome-focused:[35]

- performance anxiety increases
- cognitive capability reduces
- loss aversion increases
- a tendency to focus on outcomes with higher certainty arises (ambiguity aversion)
- overcollection and use of data, both useful and useless, increases.

A continued over-obsessive outcome focus can also reduce innovation, learning and risk-taking. None of which is desirable. These are three qualities which are particularly important to surviving changing markets over time.

What is the solution?

The answer is to develop a *stronger process focus* – to become more aware not just of the result, but *how* you got the result, and, when executing your trades, to spend less time focusing on whether you are making money or not, and more time focusing on the task that is most important in that moment: taking the actions that are required to maximise your chances of success.

PROCESS FOCUS

Trading is an activity where the outcome of your trade is a result of your process, your trading skill, and luck. Yes, luck, or if you are more comfortable with it: *randomness*.

This has strong implications for how you approach your trading, specifically the importance of focusing on your *trading process* – the specific steps you take to maximise your chances of success instead of getting obsessed about your results and outcomes (or 'resulting' as it is called in Poker).

Process + luck = outcome

When luck is involved in any activity, the relationship between cause and effect is broken. In a pure skill-based activity – for example, playing the violin – if you practise effectively you will get better in the short term and over time. There is high cause and effect correlation. Quality, deliberate practice leads to improved playing ability. When luck is involved you can do everything right – in trading terms, follow your process and execute your strategy effectively – but the outcome can be bad in the short term. You can lose.

And, conversely, you can do everything wrong – be ill-disciplined and not follow your process – and get a good outcome. A win.

A simple example of this from the casino would be playing blackjack and being dealt 17. The highest probability move here is to stay with 17. In the long term this will be the most effective way to reduce your losses to the edge of the house. However, imagine instead that you ask for a hit and get dealt a 4. You now have 21 and win. This is an example of a bad process leading to a good outcome – you win in the short term, but if you sustained that same strategy in the long term you would lose.

Process vs outcome

	Win	Lose
Good process	Deserved success	Bad break
Bad process	Dumb luck	Poetic justice

Source: *Winning Decisions*, Russo and Schoemaker

The relationship between process and outcome can be seen in this table from the book *Winning Decisions*.[36] It is possible to follow your trading process and win or lose, and likewise to not follow your trading process and win or lose. The probability of success will be greater, purely on a statistical level, when you are able to trade your process consistently (assuming you have a trading process/strategy with an edge). But it will also be greater due to the different psychological experience and benefits of being process-focused.

A process focus is key to success in probabilistic performance domains such as trading. It has several advantages over being more results-focused, including:

- reduces performance stress, anxiety and emotion-driven decision-making

- engages the deliberate mind and reduces mental blind spots

- enables you to clearly focus on what is important

- enhances the ability to improve your decision-making over time.

FROM P&L-FOCUSED TO PROCESS-FOCUSED

"When I see an anxious person, I ask myself, what do they want?
For if a person wasn't wanting something outside of their own
control, why would they be stricken by anxiety?"

– Epictetus

I first met John for coaching one September, as a part of a programme I was running for a desk of FX traders at an investment bank. We were a couple of sessions into the programme before we really got into something that John felt would be helpful for him in his trading. He had been trading for seven years and was a consistently high performer. However, he faced one serious challenge. It is one that many institutional traders have. And that is: coping with the P&L reset at the end of the trading year, in his case 31 December, and the subsequent start of the new year with a P&L of zero. This became the focus for our sessions.

Many traders feel more pressure to make money when their P&L is zero compared to when there is money on the board. Losing money when you have some in the bank feels also less bad for many traders than when you lose the same amount of money from zero. For John this sense of pressure was manifesting as a risk-averse defensive trading style early in the year (until there were runs on the board), with an underlying anxiety and fear of losing. In recent years he had also developed an eye-twitch – fascinatingly, it was only present from the start of the year until he had made sufficient P&L. Typically, some time in Q2, it vanished.

Through our sessions we focused, firstly, on awareness: on how his decision-making was being affected by his shift in focus away from trading the market and making good decisions, towards trading his P&L and trying not to lose money.

We explored the different point of focus in each situation: the thoughts, feelings and sensations that he was aware of for each, and the action he was taking, and the impact of this action in both the short and long term.

John was deeply P&L focused from 1 January. With a few months of work together, from about October through to the end of December, we decided to work on becoming more process-focused. Not to ignore the P&L. But to be less attached to it. To get into how he was making or losing money, not just *how much* he was making or losing.

Ultimately the new focus was on making good trading decisions.

Over the weeks, through his own journaling process, reflecting on how he made decisions and the factors that affected those decisions, he made a shift away from being deeply attached to the outcome, to having a strong curiosity about his decision-making process and related factors.

This new approach was seriously tested at the beginning of December when he got caught in a market move against him. In an illiquid market, it left him with a big loss right before the end of the trading year, significantly impacting his P&L and his bonus. What was interesting was that he reported that even though this was a "pretty big loss" (millions), he felt he had responded well. He had kept his head. Focused on making good decisions. Didn't get carried away with the emotions that come with losing money and the reactive decisions they could lead to.

He had been able to minimise his losses compared to what they might have been.

He was naturally frustrated with the outcome, the impact on his P&L and the timing of it. Most traders would be. But he had experienced the impact of being decision-focused instead of money-focused at the behavioural, emotional and financial level. It was a great learning experience.

We ended our coaching work in December. I was, of course, curious to find out what would happen come January. So we agreed to meet a few weeks into the new year. What happened? Firstly, John had maintained a focus on making good decisions. There was still some anxiety at the start of the year (I would say this is normal). But less so than in previous years. And there was no eye twitch. He had had a positive start to the year P&L-wise.

The shift he experienced – from an obsession about results and outcomes, to a fascination with the process of making good trading decisions – was quite dramatic.

BECOMING MORE PROCESS-FOCUSED

There are several actions you can take to become more process-focused. I stress *more* process focused, not becoming *entirely* process-focused; I am not advocating you completely ignore your P&L. It's about getting a better balance.

1. Make a decision to become more process-focused as a part of your mindset as a bulletproof trader. See and understand the importance of focusing on your trading process. Make it a principle of your approach to the markets.

2. Set an intention to focus on becoming a better decision maker and improving your decision-making process in particular. If you become better at making trading decisions you will increase your chances of achieving your full trading potential.

3. Develop your interest and curiosity in the relationship between your trading process, the markets and the outcomes you get. When evaluating your trading decisions don't just focus on 'what' the outcome was, focus much more on 'how' you made the decision, the actions you took, how you were thinking and feeling, what the context was.

4. Become aware of when you find yourself overly focusing on your P&L or your results, either wins or losses. Take a long slow deep breath. Ask 'What is important for me to focus on now?'

5. For some traders a checklist is a way to have a physical anchor to the trading process, and a reminder of actions to take/questions to ask in specific stages of the trade cycle. Checklists place an emphasis on task focus.

13

CONTROL THE CONTROLLABLES

UNCONTROLLABILITY, STRESS AND THE MARKETS

IN A RESEARCH study, two animals were given shocks and their responses were monitored. One animal had access to a bar lever that could stop the shock for both of them, providing it with an element of control; the other didn't. At the end of the experiment both animals had been exposed to an identical amount of shock. However, the animal which had not had access to a lever had experienced a much greater stress response.

This (perhaps somewhat cruel) study illustrates the relationship between stress and control. When we feel in control we have a lower response to stress; when we feel less in control we have a higher response.

Control – even an illusion of it – can mitigate the stress response. Uncontrollability is stressful, and along with uncertainty and novelty is one of the three situations that can elicit significant physiological stress responses.

The trading environment exposes traders to this trinity of stressors on a daily basis. In his research with traders, John Coates monitored traders' P&L on a daily basis, assessing its variability using this as a measure of control.[37] He took saliva samples from the traders to assess their hormonal states, particularly looking at testosterone and the stress hormone cortisol. Coates found that, as traders' P&L variability increased (i.e. as uncontrollability increased), so did their cortisol levels.

> "During a drawdown, wanting to reduce position sizes but not being able to, is very stressful. This is a real problem in credit markets where liquidity (your ability to buy or, more importantly, sell an asset) can disappear in an instant."
>
> **– A fund manager**

THE DICHOTOMY OF CONTROL

'Control the controllables' has become a sports and performance psychology mantra, even a cliché. But it is solid advice that is absolutely essential to performing at your best – both in the moment and over time as a trader.

A focus on what is controllable, as we have seen, reduces the stress response – which frees up mental and physical resources (capacity), and allows you to allocate them to where there is greater bang for buck: on the execution of your trading process.

The idea of controlling the controllables is not a new one. In fact, it is (again) a key principle of Stoic philosophy. The ability to differentiate between what can be controlled and what cannot be controlled, and what can be changed and what cannot be changed, was at the heart of Stoic practice.

"The chief task in life is simply this: to identify and separate matters so that I can say clearly to myself which are externals not under my control, and which have to do with the choices I actually control. Where then do I look for good and evil? Not to uncontrollable externals, but within myself to the choices that are my own."

– Epictetus

A more widely known version of the same principle is that of the *serenity prayer*, popular in addiction-recovery programmes:

"God, grant me the serenity to accept the things I cannot change, the courage to change the things I can, and the wisdom to know the difference."

The concepts are the same – to recognise and then to focus on what is under your control.

Dr Suzanne Kobasa's work on developing stress hardiness reveals control as one of three key elements – alongside commitment and challenge.[38] There are two types of control: internal and external.

- People who have an *internal locus of control* know that they can't control all of the external events that happen to them in their life and in trading, but they *do* feel that they have a choice as to how they respond to those events.

- People with an *external locus of control* believe that they have little control over what happens to them – a more fatalistic approach.

An internal locus of control helps to mitigate the stress response. An extreme example of this can be found in the writings of Dr Viktor Frankl, a psychiatrist who was imprisoned in Auschwitz. In his book, *Man's Search For Meaning*,[39] he talks about how man's last freedom is his ability to choose how to deal with the situations, no matter how difficult, that life throws at him – a view shared by Epictetus: "A podium and a prison is each a place, one high and the other low, but in either place your freedom of choice can be maintained if you so wish" (*Discourses*, 2.6.25).

A SPEEDBOAT DRIVER JOINS THE CREW OF AN OIL TANKER

Matthew was an experienced trader who had taken a new role as a fund manager at a large investment firm. He had a pretty unique position within the firm, an investment manager known for its classical long-only fundamental focus. That's because Matthew was a short-term trader with a technical bias.

He was, in essence, a speedboat driver joining the crew of an oil tanker.

We met for coaching a few months into his new role. The goal was to maximise his potential and help him perform at his best. Nothing was wrong, nothing was broken. He was one of the 20% or so of clients I work with who are already doing well and simply want to do better.

It was not long into our work together before a major challenge arose. Matthew was a trader committed to producing the best possible results; he wanted to do a good job so that he could feel satisfied with himself; he also wanted, at some level, to justify his unique hire by generating returns for the firm, and in particular his boss, who had taken the risk of hiring him.

But the firm was being slow in getting his trading set-up organised. Important equipment and technology was still not available. There were key markets he simply couldn't trade. Risk limits were not in place. The pace of implementation was overwhelmingly slow; everything was bureaucratic. He became increasingly frustrated and stressed.

In one coaching session we touched on everything he saw as holding him back. I could sense his increasing exasperation. We listed everything he felt he needed to help him trade at his best – both internal factors and external factors. We then assessed what was in place already, and what was not yet in place.

The next task I gave him was to put a *C*, *I* or *A* next to each of the items:

- **C** for I can **control** this

- **I** for I can **influence** it

- **A** for I **accept** that I cannot control this at this time.

We used this template to decide where best to allocate his time and energy. It's something we talk about today, many years later, due to the impact it had on reducing his stress levels and improving his performance.

THE CIA FRAMEWORK

The CIA framework is one I often use with my clients to help them recognise the factors they have control over and those they do not.

Identifying the factors that you can and cannot control within your trading is very important. As we have seen, even an illusion of being in control mitigates the stress response, which will facilitate better cognitive functioning and enhanced decision-making.

Identifying what is controllable and what is not also allows you to focus your efforts on the areas of your trading that matter most – those that bring you the greatest returns.

Where your attention goes, so your energy flows. The same is true of time and expertise. These are three key resources, and where you focus them influences how well you perform.

The CIA framework and your resources

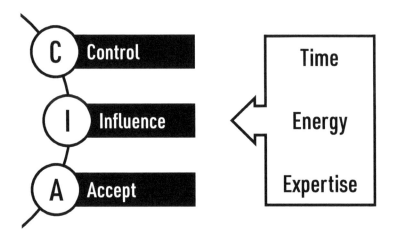

It can be a useful exercise to consider what your own CIAs are in your trading. It has always been time well spent with the many traders I have coached over the years. Ideally, of course, you would look at this within the broader context of developing your trading process.

My trading CIAs

Control	
Influence	
Accept	

WITH CONTROLLABILITY COMES RESPONSIBILITY – AND RESPONSE-ABILITY

With controllability also comes a sense of responsibility. When you have an external locus of control and believe that things are happening to you and there is nothing you can do about it, it is easy to cast off any sense of responsibility for your own decision-making.

It's like being in a yacht in the ocean in difficult conditions, and passively waiting for the storm to pass – not trimming the sails, steering the rudder or taking any action that might be helpful. If you end up in the wrong port, well, it wasn't your fault – it was the weather.

Once you start to work with an awareness of the dichotomy of control and adopt a more *internal* locus of control – focusing on what you can control, and undertaking the most helpful actions possible within that limitation – then you are also taking a greater level of responsibility. You are owning your behaviour, your trading decisions and your trading results.

This is no bad thing. There are always actions that you can take that can improve your trading situation, however bad it may seem; but unless you take responsibility for your performance, it is hard to enact them.

Knowing what you can control and what you can't control allows you to develop your 'response-ability'. As we saw earlier in the book, the uncertainty of the markets will always mean there are events outside of your control. You cannot control them. But you can control how you respond to them – your response-ability.

In challenging and difficult trading circumstances, good things start to happen when you focus on what is under your control as opposed to what is not.

PART
SIX

DISCOMFORT

14

GET COMFORTABLE WITH BEING UNCOMFORTABLE

THE DISCOMFORTS OF TRADING

S ENSATIONS OF DISCOMFORT are a common experience for anyone trading the markets. They come in many different forms, as a result of a wide variety of events and situations. Including:

- taking a loss

- holding a winning trade

- increased market volatility

- a losing run/drawdown

- being in a losing trade

- missing out on an opportunity

- quiet markets – boredom

- making a mistake

- not capitalising on a good trading opportunity

- being wrong

- a change in market conditions

- not performing as well as your peers

- investor redemptions

- uncertainty

- novel and unexpected events.

As I mentioned earlier, these are inherent to the practice of trading the markets and cannot be removed. So you have two choices. You can do your best to avoid these events and situations and the discomfort they bring, and accept the negative impact that this will likely have on your market returns. Or you can develop your ability to be comfortable with them, and increase the chances of maximising your returns.

AVERSION AND THE COSTS OF AVOIDING DISCOMFORT

Paul traded at a major hedge fund in London and had a strong edge in the market that involved identifying and getting into trades early, ahead of the majority of the competition. But in doing so he often had to endure discomfort from seeing the market move against him, or not moving as he had expected – before eventually going in the direction he anticipated.

To maximise his returns over the long run, he had to be willing to be uncomfortable in the short run.

When faced with uncomfortable situations in trading there is always a choice – avoid it or accept it and work with it. Loss aversion, regret aversion, the fear of being wrong, ambiguity aversion, fear of missing out and boredom trading are outcomes of traders avoiding discomfort. The avoidance of discomfort is normal. It's completely human. It also will not maximise your market returns.

"The human tendency to select comfortable choices will lead most to experience worse than random results."

– William Eckhardt

One of the core psychological challenges that traders face is managing the short-term discomfort that appears in many different trading situations in order to reap the long-term gains of their strategy.

Traders are often faced with a choice of doing what feels good and comfortable (avoiding pain, feeling pleasure) versus doing what matters, which can be uncomfortable. Many traders sacrifice their long-term gains for short-term comfort.

Avoiding discomfort in the short term can reduce longer-term returns

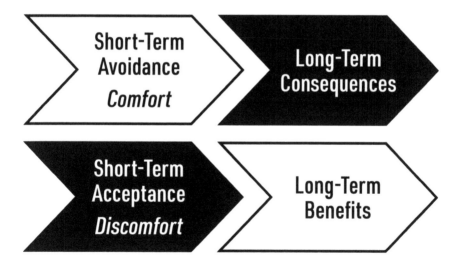

Examples of the costs of avoiding discomfort

Behaviour	Short-term comfort	Long-term consequences
Avoided pulling the trigger after a previous losing trade.	Avoided another losing trade, felt less anxious.	Missed out on a good trading opportunity and profit, felt frustrated.
Exited a profitable trade before getting to my profit target to avoid losing what I had made on the trade already.	Stopped worrying about losing the profit I had made in the trade, and how I would feel if the market retraced.	Market continued to move in my direction and I lost out on a decent amount of profit in the trade, felt pissed off.

- What thoughts, emotions and sensations are you avoiding (or would you like to get rid of) in your own trading?

- What are you doing/have you tried to do to avoid them/get rid of them?

- What are/have been the costs of this avoidance?

THE UPSIDE OF DISCOMFORT

Both psychologically and physiologically, it is quite reasonable to say that, if something difficult doesn't kill you, it makes you stronger. Or, at least, it has the potential to.

Two of the key goals of this book are to:

1. help you become more resilient to the stress response, developing your stress capacity and physiological toughness

2. help you develop the psychological skills required to cope with stressful events, difficulty and setbacks.

Neither of these is achieved through the avoidance of stress, challenge, discomfort or difficulty. On the contrary, these physiological adaptions and psychological skills are forged through *exposure* to stress and difficulty.

Your body gets good at stress by being exposed to stress. This physiological effect – the *exposure effect* – was demonstrated in a study with FX traders. Their stress response was tracked in line with changes in market volatility.[40] The more experienced traders in the study showed a lower level of stress in response to increased market volatility than newer traders in the study. Through years of experience, and exposure to market volatility, the older traders had become conditioned to the stresses of these events – adapted to them – and were now demonstrating much lower reactions as result.

Likewise, you develop the psychological skills required to cope with stressful, difficult and challenging trading situations through exposure to them. You can read about how to cope with such situations, learn techniques and strategies, and develop plans of action (as you are doing by reading this book). But the real benefit will come from the application of them when it really matters.

In order to benefit from the upsides of discomfort, and to be able to maximise your market returns, you need to get comfortable with being uncomfortable – to expose yourself to discomfort, which means being willing to accept uncomfortable thoughts, feelings and sensations.

WILLINGNESS: EXPOSURE IN ACTION

If you do not want to suffer from the reduced P&L brought about by loss aversion, regret aversion, the fear of being wrong, boredom, ambiguity aversion, fear of missing out and the other aversive behaviours that traders demonstrate, then what is the alternative?

The alternative to avoidance is willingness and acceptance. *Not* in a passive, resigned way – and also not in a 'tolerating' way. But being open and willing to accept the discomfort of the internal experiences that come with losing, making mistakes, missing out, being wrong and many other trading situations. You don't have to like the experience. You don't have to want it or approve of it in order to be willing to accept it. It is about letting go of the struggle to *avoid* these internal events.

Developing the willingness to be open to discomfort (difficult emotions, thoughts and sensations) is one of the most fundamental shifts a trader can make in developing his or her psychological capacity to deal with stressful, challenging and difficult events. In combination with taking committed action this is a fundamental factor in trading discipline – and in getting through tough trading periods.

It is important to state that the intention behind cultivating willingness to feel difficult thoughts, emotions and sensations *is in order to allow you to take effective trading action*. It's something that frees you up to take the specific steps required to stack the odds of success in your favour.

Willingness requires you to be open to make room for uncomfortable thoughts, emotions and sensations – even to lean into them. Fully experience them. Accept them as they are. With increased willingness you can move from loss aversion to loss acceptance; from ambiguity aversion to ambiguity acceptance; from regret aversion to regret acceptance. All of which can make a significant difference to your trading behaviour, decision-making and market returns.

One of the most important benefits of developing your willingness to accept – and even seek out – challenging and difficult experiences is that it will provide exposure to them. Which brings both physiological and psychological benefits that are central to developing your stress capacity, toughness and resilience.

Willingness is exposure in action.

> • What are the specific behaviours and actions that you need to take that are likely to result in you trading at your best and achieving your full trading potential?
>
> • Are you willing to accept the difficult internal experiences that may show up as you take action towards achieving your trading goals?

DEVELOPING WILLINGNESS: GETTING GOOD AT DISCOMFORT

Willingness and acceptance happen at many different levels:

• Being willing to accept the reality of trading for what it is. No matter how hard, challenging and difficult it may be at that time. Not wishing for it to be different. Simply taking whatever the effective action may be.

> "Don't seek for everything to happen as you wish it would, but rather wish that everything happens as it actually will – then your life will flow well."
>
> **– Epictetus**

• Being willing to accept what you can and what you cannot control in your trading. And that attempts to control or get rid of your difficult internal experiences may actually make them worse and adversely affect your trading decisions and results.

> "The chief task in life is simply this: to identify and separate matters so that I can say clearly to myself which are externals not under my control, and which have to do with the choices I actually control. Where then do I look for good and evil? Not to uncontrollable externals, but within myself to the choices that are my own."
>
> – Epictetus

- Being willing to accept uncomfortable and difficult thoughts, emotions and sensations that show up. Being able to be with them, lean into them, while keeping a focus on taking committed and effective action for the situation you are in.

> "Objective judgement, now at this very moment. Unselfish action, now at this very moment. Willing acceptance, now at this very moment, of all external events. That's all you need."
>
> – Marcus Aurelius

One client I worked with had what he referred to as a "game-changing moment" in one particular coaching session. We were discussing uncomfortable thoughts, emotions and sensations he had been feeling about his trading. What made the breakthrough was when I told him that everything he was experiencing *was exactly what I had heard from other traders*. It was not just him; discomfort was part of the trading experience. Furthermore, these discomforts were perfectly normal – part of the human condition.

When you see discomfort as normal, it changes your relationship with it. You become less averse – and, as a result, more resilient. You make better decisions.

PRACTISING WILLINGNESS AND DISCOMFORT

Cato, one of the better-known Stoics, was financially well off and had the resources to dress well. But he often chose to walk around Rome in barefoot. Many Stoics, despite being rich and powerful, likewise chose to live simple or rough lives on some days of the week.

The purpose of this behaviour was to practise difficulty.

Practising difficulty helps us to become stronger and more resilient. We get comfortable with discomfort. The Stoics were training themselves to be able to cope with a variety of different conditions. They recognised that discomfort was a part of life, and that the only way to get good at anything was to practise it.

Another way in which the Stoics practised difficulty was *negative visualisation* – imagining themselves in difficult situations. If any of the envisioned events should happen, they were then able to deal with them with greater equanimity. This is similar to modern psychological approaches such as *stress-inoculation training*, where people spend time visualising difficult situations and practising their coping skills, and how they might respond. These are mental training strategies that I often utilise with my own trading clients in order to help them to practise, and get comfortable with, discomfort.

Here is a quick example of a practice you could use to rehearse being open and willing to accept discomfort in your own trading.

Bring to mind a stressful, difficult or challenging situation that you experience in your trading – something uncomfortable for you.

- Notice what thoughts, emotions and physical sensations show up.

- Notice any impulses, urges or attempts to try to get rid of them.

- Instead, see if you are able to open up – accept them as they are in that moment. Stay with the discomfort. There is no need for anything to be any different.

You can develop the practice further by adding the action you would like to take in that situation – something in line with your trading goals, values and process.

- Bring to mind a strength or quality that you would like to demonstrate in this situation or event.

- In your mind, imagine taking the effective action you would like to take in this situation. Trade your process. Perform with poise.

15

UNHOOK FROM DIFFICULT THOUGHTS

THINKING ABOUT YOUR THINKING

WHAT THOUGHTS, WORRIES, self-criticisms, memories or other unhelpful thoughts do you get caught up in that interfere with your trading decisions and results?

Traders spend a lot of their time thinking about their trading, about their positions, about other traders. And, of course, about the markets. And all of these both during and after market hours.

Sometimes these thoughts are helpful. They drive effective action which adds to the trader's experience. Sometimes these thoughts are less helpful. Traders get too wrapped up in them. They become hooked – and the result is they engage in behaviour that reduces their trading returns.

Due to the challenges involved in trading the markets, it is natural to expect difficult thoughts to show up. As we have covered, this is the human condition. It is how the mind works.

How you deal with these thoughts has a significant impact on the decisions you make – and the returns you get.

> "On occasion I have suffered from acute bouts of anxiety caused by this job. The most destructive thoughts concern unreasonable feelings of negativity towards my own abilities and process. For example, despite generating circa $500m of career P&L (of which $100m came last year), losing $20m this year has caused me to question whether I'm good enough to do this job. On one level I know this is irrational... but it doesn't stop me thinking this on an almost daily basis."
>
> **– A fund manager**

The quote above is a good example from a successful fund manager I worked with. It illustrates exactly how our thoughts can impact us.

I have heard many successful traders and fund managers question whether they are good enough – often while sitting on a pile of evidence that confirms they are.

But the mind is fickle. It is easily swayed by what is recent and threatening. Recent losses dominate over longer-term performance because the stress response focuses our attention and thinking on the short term. Irrational doubts about our abilities arise. We can struggle to reason our way out of them.

DON'T THINK OF A WHITE BEAR

Take five minutes. Sit still and quiet. And try not to think about a white bear.

Every time you catch yourself thinking about a white bear, make a note somewhere. Keep score.

How many times did you think about a white bear?

The above exercise is taken from a study conducted by Daniel Wegner in 1987 which focused on *thought suppression* – what happens when you try not to think of something.[41] In Wegner's study, the participants were asked to use suppression techniques to avoiding thinking about a white bear and to ring a bell if they did have a thought about it during the five minutes.

The study found that using suppression strategies to resist thinking about the white bear *increased the frequency of thinking about the white bear*, a phenomenon know as 'ironic mental procesing'. What is interesting is that this effect was even more pronounced in the time immediately following the experiment.

Suppression and control strategies may not be the most effective way to manage your mind as a trader, particularly where there is exposure to multiple stressors and difficult situations. Suppression is also metabolically demanding. It requires energy, drains brain resources, and takes your focus away from the task at hand.

LETTING GO OF THE STRUGGLE

"I can't get out now."

"The market will come back."

"You can't afford to take that loss."

"You need this trade to be a winner."

These are some of the thoughts that Rakesh, a client of mine, typically has when faced with taking a loss. Especially if he has had a previous losing trade or is in a run of losses.

Rakesh's strategy for managing his mind was to try to ignore his thoughts. To not think them. Or to try and think something else instead – something more positive. These are typical ways of managing our thinking; you may recognise them from your own thoughts.

The result was that he felt he was in a constant struggle with his thoughts. In his own words it was "a battle" – and it was tiring.

Many traders I work with struggle with unhelpful thoughts that show up in their trading. At times of difficulty and stress, it is likely that such things occur. It's normal – to some extent it is the brain doing its job. It doesn't really matter if they occur – what matters is how you manage them.

Working with difficult thoughts requires the development of four key mental skills:

1. Awareness – of your thoughts *as* thoughts.

2. Workability – is a thought helpful or not in context?

3. Defusion – learning how to 'unhook' from difficult and unhelpful thoughts.

4. Action – taking committed action; following your process.

1. AWARENESS

Before you can effectively manage your mind, you need to be aware of your thoughts as you are thinking them; in the moment. This is why focused attention training practices and developing present moment awareness are so important.

Here is a simple exercise you can practise to train your ability to notice your thinking. What we're doing here is building your metacognition.

Close your eyes and simply notice what your mind does. Observe any thoughts or images that arise without looking for them. If no thoughts or images appear, that is OK; just keep watching.

- You might like to label your thoughts: e.g., 'planning', 'worrying', 'judging'.

- Notice that a part of you is thinking, while another part of you is *observing* you thinking.

This exercise has two benefits. Firstly, it is a great way to start to bring awareness to your thoughts. Secondly, it is a key step towards enabling you to make the vital distinction between *you* and *your thoughts*.

Thoughts are mental events; they are not you, and they are not always facts.

We cannot always choose the thoughts that come into our minds. But we *can* choose how much attention we give them, and how we relate to them.

Seeing thoughts as thoughts – as mental events – allows you to experience your thoughts differently. You can relate to them in a different way. And you can manage them effectively, reducing their impact on taking action, on trading your process, on taking the actions that stack the odds of success in your favour.

2. WORKABILITY

When we look at our thinking it is common to think about it in terms of being positive or negative. However, positivity or negativity is a function of the context you are in. It is more useful to look at thoughts under the lens of *workability*.

Is this thought helping me take effective trading action, in line with my process, values and goals?

If yes, it is workable and there is nothing to do. If the thought is inhibiting effective action then it is not workable – and may need to be managed.

In any given context, a thought can be helpful or not, workable or not. Moving away from a positive/negative focus gives you a much stronger grasp of the function of your thinking. It also increases your mental flexibility – it's a far more agile approach to managing your mind.

3. DEFUSION

"It's impossible to make money in these markets."

Imagine if you, like a client of mine, had that thought. And not just had it – but believed it emphatically. So much so you couldn't see any way past it.

This is known as being *fused* (in simpler terms 'hooked'). How would it affect your trading behaviour? Perhaps you might notice some stress and anxiety; a sense of being resigned to not making money; a feeling that it might not even be worth making the effort to do so. And a curious tendency to take unhelpful courses of action.

The thought 'It's impossible to make money in these markets' is, though, just a thought. And it is not the thought itself that is problematic – it is being caught up in this thought; being fused to it.

Cognitive fusion is when we see thoughts as fixed and established truths that cannot be changed. They are rules to obey; or threats that must be avoided; or something that is happening and which cannot be stopped. And always something of the utmost importance.

Cognitive defusion recognises that thoughts may or may not be true – that they are not a command or a rule you have to follow. They may or may not be important. And they can be allowed to come and go.

The difference between being fused with a thought, and defused, is significant in its impact on trading behaviour.

Try this quick exercise to get a sense of the difference between being hooked or not, and the process of unhooking.

- Think about a challenging situation that you experience in your trading and a difficult thought that shows up.

- Write it down as large as possible on a piece of A4 paper.

- Bring the paper close to your face. Right in front of you. Take a moment to notice what this is like for you.

- Now move the paper to an arm's-length distance. Take a moment to notice what this is like for you.

- Now place the paper on your lap. Take a moment to notice what this is like for you.

Compare the three experiences.

Typical reflections from my clients following this exercise include observations that when the paper (the thought) is up close it is hard to see much else. It dominates the experience. At arm's-length there is a distancing from the thought. It feels less intense. However, it takes some effort to hold it there. On the lap there is an awareness that the thought is there – but it does not dominate your experience. And it does not require the effort that holding it at arm's-length does.

The simplest and most basic of defusion strategies is just to notice your thoughts as thoughts, as mental events – not as facts, commands, truths or rules that must be obeyed. By making this shift you are immediately disentangling from your thinking.

When you become aware of a thought that may not be workable in your trading you can also apply the following simple defusion strategies:

Preface the thought with 'I am thinking...' or 'I am noticing I am thinking...' or even 'I am noticing that my mind is thinking...', e.g.

- 'I am thinking that the markets are impossible to trade'
- 'I am noticing I am thinking the markets are impossible to trade'
- 'I am noticing my mind is thinking the markets are impossible to trade'

Say the thought very slowly and deliberately.

Write the thought down.

Keeping a trading journal where you write down your trades *as well as your thoughts* about your trades allows for defusion to occur naturally. The process of writing down your thoughts enables you to recognise them as thoughts – and to see them from a distance.

In coaching I often get clients to write their thoughts on a flipchart, and then get them to look at their thoughts, take a few steps back and look at them again. The content of the thoughts never change – but how they experience them and relate to them does.

4. ACTION

It is important to finish by reminding you that the purpose of managing your thoughts is to allow you to sustain a focus on taking the actions that you need to take to maximise your chances of success in the markets – to execute your trading process as consistently and as effectively as is possible.

Action is always at the core of how well you trade.

> From a sitting position say to yourself, repeatedly, 'sit down'. And while doing so, stand up. Then from your standing position, say to yourself repeatedly 'stand up'. And while doing so, sit down.
>
> This simple exercise helps prove to yourself it is perfectly possible to have a thought and to behave in a way that is contrary to that thought, especially if you are not hooked by that thought.

You can hold the thought *'I am worried about losing money, I need to get out of this trade'* and still stay in the trade if that is what your process dictates, providing you have the awareness to notice the thought, are able to accept and unhook – *'I am noticing that my mind is thinking I am worried about losing money, and that I need to get out of this trade'* – and you are committed to the execution of your process.

16

WORK WITH YOUR STRESS-BASED EMOTIONS

TRADING, LIKE LIFE, IS EMOTIONAL

"Anger and frustration are two of the most destructive emotions
I experience in my trading. Nothing annoys me more than poor
trading performance or underachieving – when I don't perform,
it can be very frustrating, which in turn results in impulsive
decisions or just wrong trading decisions."

– A proprietary trader

LIFE IS EMOTIONAL. So is trading. Trading the markets exposes traders to the highs and lows of the human experience – and these can be very high and very low. From euphoria, excitement and joy – to fear, anxiety, anger, frustration, sadness and despair.

Think back on your own trading. What emotions have you experienced?

A TRADER WORKS WITH ANXIETY

David was a trader at a leading investment bank. Twelve months before we met he had moved to the UK to head up an emerging markets trading desk. Prior to this he had about 15 years of market experience successfully trading his home currency against the dollar. He had built up a deep expertise in his market and was a valued source of information to other traders. His motivation in moving to London had been a combination of the professional and the personal.

David contacted me for coaching because his trading performance had fallen below his own expectations. He had a strong commitment to being the best trader he could; he was also concerned with how this was being perceived by his team – and his manager.

There were two key challenges at the core of David's new role:

1. managing a trading team for the first time

2. producing good P&L in his own trading book, including trading some emerging market currencies he had not traded before.

The manager-producer role is a challenging one in itself – with pressure to get the best out of others *and* out of yourself. David had added to it by wanting to prove to himself and to others that he was a good hire.

In one of our first coaching sessions we were focusing on his trading decision-making. I had asked whether he kept a trading journal so that we could review his decision-making together in future sessions.

He said that he did keep a journal of his trades – with the key market data, position size, and his stop-loss and profit targets, along with a couple of thoughts as to why he was taking a trade. But that was the only information in it.

I asked if he would be willing to add a bit more depth to this last part: to include his thoughts surrounding why he got in, any changes of mind, and why he got out. Additionally, to record any feelings he was aware of while having these thoughts.

He was onboard until we got to feelings. All the same, he agreed to give it a go. I said that just a single word would suffice.

We met again four weeks later. He pulled out his trading journal and told me he had been reflecting on what he had been writing about his feelings. He was surprised that he had written the word 'anxiety' down a lot. Anxiety was not an unfamiliar feeling for him. Its frequency, though, had been unexpected.

And he had puzzled over this. His conclusion was that his anxiety was showing up as a result of:

- worrying about managing the team and his lack of skills in being able to do so (competence)

- worrying about his results (outcome focus)

- worrying about trading new markets (competence/experience).

When he dug down into his trading what emerged was an approach that was largely based on his way of trading his core market. This was mostly short term, with a healthy dose of intuitive decision-making underpinned by a lot of experience and deep expertise. It simply did not transfer to the new markets.

The intuitive 'feel' of something is contextual. It does automatically not apply from one domain to another; it must be developed through experience.

And due to performance pressure he was taking relatively large risk in markets where he had limited experience and competence.

Armed with these insights, he decided to make some changes. He spent time learning more about the markets he was trading, developed a more systematic approach to trading them, and reduced the risk he was taking. It was not long before he noticed a reduction in his frequency of reporting feeling anxious.

Why is this important? Think about what you would do if you were experiencing anxiety in your own trading. Many people might label that as a negative emotion, find it uncomfortable and seek to get rid of it. Maybe through the use of breathing techniques; maybe even avoiding situations where the anxiety arises.

In David's situation this would have led to him either doing a lot of breathing techniques, or not trading at all. Neither would have served him well in the pursuit of trading at his best or achieving his long-term goals.

Instead, here is what David did:

- noticed the emotion and named it
- asked 'what might be behind this?'
- took action on his insights.

As a result, he reduced his anxiety and increased his performance.

WORKING WITH EMOTIONS

"Dealing with impatience and acting out of frustration has been my
biggest challenge. It has been a long process, involving becoming much
more emotionally intelligent – and better able to understand the early
signs of such feelings. Assessing myself from an emotional point of
view was the simplest but most powerful discovery I've made in trading."

– A hedge fund trader

A bulletproof trader needs to go through three stages in working with
his or her emotions. These stages are part of developing psychological
flexibility and are based on neuroscientific research into emotions and
decision-making:

1. awareness

2. acceptance/willingness

3. action.

1. AWARENESS – NOTICING AND NAMING

The first step towards being able to work with your emotions is to be
able to recognise them – to be aware of them. Remember, we're not
interested in elimination – but greater awareness.

A simple first step is to start adding information to your trading
journal about how you feel during your trading process. Record how
you are feeling:

• at the start of the day

• as you prepare trades

• when you enter the market

• as you manage your positions

- when you exit

- and when you reflect upon your trades.

One technique I often use with clients, especially those going through a difficult time, is the *daily download*. This is an end-of-day journal specifically focused on writing down thoughts and feelings after a day's trading. It provides a regular opportunity for defusion, processing and reflection.

> "One aspect that I have taken from the coaching that has made a huge difference for me has been taking time at the end of the trading day to do the daily download. Being able to get my thoughts and feelings out at the end of each day has been really helpful."
> **– A fund manager**

A second way is to start to 'check-in' – to pause during the day and ask '*What am I feeling right now?*' Perhaps write it down; at the very least name it. Research shows that when people are able to notice and name the emotion they are feeling – known as *affect labelling* – it has the effect of reducing its intensity. This naming and taming is an effective standalone technique for managing difficult emotions.

A third way to develop greater emotional awareness is by utilising mindful/awareness-type practices that help you to develop your *interoception*. This is your brain's ability to read the physiological signs in your body. Emotions are sets of physiological sensations that we have given names to. Getting good at being aware of emotions means getting good at recognising these physiological sensations. In a research study conducted at a London hedge fund, traders' interoceptive abilities were measured – and high scores on interoception were correlated with P&L, profitability and career longevity.[42]

2. ACCEPTING – EMOTIONS AS DATA

What emotions do you fight?

Stress-based survival emotions can feel uncomfortable. As a result we can end up creating aversions to them. This aversiveness can be increased when we label these emotions as negative.

It is important to remember that everything is contextual. How you feel, think and act should be a question of workability – is an emotion helpful in a given situation or not? Fear in a life-threatening situation is entirely helpful, energising your body's resources for survival. A similar response while taking a loss in the markets may be less helpful.

ACT (Acceptance Commitment Therapy) argues that the biggest problem with our emotions and our subsequent behaviour is not the emotions themselves. It's our attempts to control them. Suppressing an emotion is like a holding a beachball under water. The ball is still there. It takes effort to hold it down. And you're focused on something you're trying not focus on, rather on what is going on around you.

If we are not going to suppress our emotions, what are we going to do? Accept them. Allow them. Research shows that there is a strong relationship between a trader's emotional management strategy, trading behaviour and results.[43] Crucially, those who attempt to suppress emotions make significantly worse decisions.

If we suppress emotions we may also close ourselves off to valuable information coming in through our senses. It denies us important data about potential risks and rewards. Thinking about emotions as data is a great way to develop your openness to them. *'What could this emotion be telling me?'*

When emotions are data, all emotions are useful.

"Risk is the possibility of a loss and the magnitude of the loss. We register risk in our bodies as feelings of fear. One way to manage various forms of risk, including prospective risk, initial risk, open risk and unconscious risk is to make sure your feeling of fear is an ally, fully functioning on your emotional instrument panel. In our medicinal culture, some people attempt to mediate fear, rather than manage risk. In general people with willingness to experience fear and other feelings are better risk managers than those who have fear in knots or fear under the influence of narcotics."[44]

– Ed Seykota

Here is a practice for helping you develop emotional awareness and acceptance. It's all about "having your emotions, without your emotions having you".[45]

Settle into a relaxed and comfortable position. When you're ready, close your eyes.

Bring awareness to your breathing; be conscious of the physical sensation of your breath in your body.

When you are ready, bring an awareness to whatever feelings are present. As you become aware of them, label them – e.g. happy, sad, frustrated, excited.

Once you have noticed and named a feeling, see if you can bring an awareness to a particular feeling and where it lives in your body – your chest, belly, head? And how it feels – smooth, heavy, warm, hard, light?

Allow the emotion to be present as you experience it.

Bring the practice to an end when you're ready, shift your focus to your breath, and return your focus to the room.

3. ACTION

Understanding your emotions was a key part of Stoicism. Being emotionless – despite popular perception – was not.

Hiding your emotions simply wasn't a part of the Stoic philosophy. Their approach was more about trying to understand emotions – acknowledging them, reflecting on them, and, where possible, directing them for their own good.

The Stoics believed that it was possible to train yourself to act calmly *despite* experiencing a feeling of anger, and to act courageously *despite* feeling anxious. The goal was not to eliminate emotions – but to not get overwhelmed by them, or to be forced to act them out.

Effective trading action has to be taken in the presence of difficult emotions. Emotions may bring with them an urge to action – but you do not have to act upon that urge. Awareness of your emotions can in itself significantly soften the urge to act them out. Always remember, emotions do not cause losses (or wins) – actions do.

What emotions are you willing to accept in the service of taking action in line with your trading goals, values and process?

PART
SEVEN

CONFIDENCE

17

BUILD CONFIDENCE IN COPING WITH DIFFICULTY

WHAT IS CONFIDENCE?

Here are two definitions of confidence:

1. A feeling of certainty or assurance.

2. An act of trust or reliance.

Which one would you choose?

The first is by far the most popular. Most traders think about confidence as a powerful feeling – being composed, a sense of knowing that you will trade well and make money, an absence of fear, anxiety, self-doubt or other negative thoughts.

The second definition is different. It places the focus on action. This definition is rooted in its ancient Latin origins, with the word *confidence* being derived from 'com' meaning with, and 'fidre' meaning trust – *with trust*.

When you make a trade in the markets, can you really expect to have feelings of absolute certainty about the outcome of a decision – when, by definition, you are taking a risk under conditions of uncertainty and uncontrollability?

Making a trade is an act of trust. You are trusting in your strategy. And you are trusting in yourself to execute it. It is normal not to have feelings of absolute assurance when making a trade. There is no guarantee of a positive outcome.

But a bulletproof confidence is focused on building trust in yourself and your trading system: on taking action, on executing your strategy, even when thoughts, emotions and sensations make it difficult to do so. It has a strong focus on developing trust that you can cope with the demands of trading. It has a reliance on mental and physical resources to deal with stresses, setbacks, losses, drawdown, mistakes and other challenges.

Confidence is built through action. Becoming confident at anything is a result of practice and experience. Experience and skill form the backbone of a trader's confidence. Developing and testing and trading your strategy will build trust and confidence in it. Facing difficult trading situations and working your way through them will develop your coping skills. Confidence in the bulletproof framework is not so much about expecting the best – but about building the resources so that you are able to deal with the worst.

DEMANDS VS RESOURCES

Psychologists have found that the most important factor in determining your response to a pressure situation is not the situation itself, but how you think about your ability to deal with it. Your brain makes an assessment of the demands of the challenge you are facing. Then it assesses whether you have the resources to face it.

How hard is this going to be?

Do I have the skills, the strength, the resources to cope? Is there anyone who could help me?

Demands vs resources

Demands > Resources = Threat
Demands < Resources = Challenge

If the brain assesses that the demands you are facing outweigh your resources then a threat response is activated. If, however, your brain assesses that you have sufficient resources to meet the demands then a challenge response if activated.

Research has shown that in many high-stakes situations a challenge response predicts better performance under pressure than a threat response. Students with a high challenge response score higher on exams; business negotiators make better decisions; surgeons show better focus and fine motor skills; athletes perform better in competition; pilots perform better in simulated engine failures.[46] Having the resources to meet the demands of a challenge is key to performing in high-stakes situations.

I often think about this relationship and its impact on confidence like a pile of poker chips. The more poker chips you have in your pile the more confident you will feel in taking on a challenge. With a bigger pile of chips you can take on more, and bigger, challenges. With fewer chips, when you are 'short stacked', you have less resources to take on challenges – and are likely to be more cautious and risk averse.

The more chips, the greater the confidence to face challenges

A very useful ongoing practice that traders can adopt is to find ways to grow their poker chip stack – to develop practices that build the resources required to cope with the demands of trading the markets. This will allow them to benefit from engaging the challenge response, rather than being thrown into the threat response.

I CAN DEAL WITH DIFFICULT TRADING SITUATIONS

"For every challenge, remember the resources you have
within you to cope with it."

– Epictetus

One of the key goals of this book is to help you build your inner citadel, such that you can more effectively cope with challenges the market presents to you. I want you to be able to say to yourself, and mean it, '*I can cope with difficult trading situations*'.

To be clear: merely saying it, as some kind of motivational affirmation, is not effective. That is not what this is about. I want you to be able to say it because it is true – and that means that it must be supported by evidence. You must have the resources and experience to back it up.

"I know that some of my best trading has come after losses or
drawdowns. That is one of my strengths – making back drawdowns
relatively quickly so I know that and count on it. I know I do very well
under pressure, especially since I have so much experience now."

– A hedge fund trader

Here are some ways in which you can build your own confidence resources and create an evidence base that allows you to say 'I can cope with difficult trading situations' and, justly, believe it – because it's true.

Acknowledge personal strengths

Reflect on your strengths and qualities as a trader. Write them down. In a difficult moment bring a relevant strength or quality to mind, and express how it can help you.

Think about how you have prepared for a particular situation

Remind yourself of how you have prepared for a moment. It could be through past market experiences, or how you prepared for a trade (including research and trade planning, scenario analysis and pre-mortem).

Remember times when you have overcome similar challenges

This is probably the most important of all. Being bulletproof is built through experience. It's a result of every tough moment in the market, every loss, mistake, setback and period of drawdown you have encountered. They've all helped you become better at dealing with these situations.

Remind yourself of some of the challenges and difficulties you have already overcome in your trading, what skills and strategies you developed as a result, and what these experiences taught you.

Support – who can help me?

While resilience is often talked about as an individual attribute, research demonstrates that support is one of the key factors in what enables a person to be resilient. It is useful to think about who is in your own support network: fellow traders, a coach or mentor, a friend, family members?

What strengths and qualities do these people have that you can 'tap into' when needed?

In the following table, consider some of the common challenges you face, or might face, within your trading. Record some of the coping resources you have available to help you deal with them.

The core focus of this process is developing an evidence-based set of resources so that when you say to yourself 'I can deal with this difficult situation' it will be true; you will believe it; and you will feel more confident as a result.

Situation	Strength	Past challenge	Support
What is the event or situation?	What strength can you leverage in this situation?	Examples of similar challenges overcome in the past.	Who could be helpful to you in this situation?

THE CONFIDENCE GAP: TAKING ACTION

'When I feel confident, I will get back into the market and trade again.'

Have you ever had that thought – or a thought like it? What happens when you have this thought – how do you feel and behave?

It's a common thought. And holding onto it too tightly can hold you back in your trading. It can have a particularly strong impact on your ability to recover from setbacks – waiting to feel confident enough following a big loss or string of losses exposes you to the significant potential of missed opportunities. The fear of losing again inhibits effective trading action. This process of allowing fear to get in the way of taking effective action is something that leading ACT practitioner Dr Russ Harris calls the *confidence gap*.[47]

Whether you are making money or losing money, just had a winning trade or a losing trade, the goal for the next moment is to take whatever action is required according to your trading process. This process we have referred to as committed action – as poise – but it is really what most traders would see as *confidence*. Taking committed action builds confidence.

> "A three-month period of drawdown this year was tough. The commitment starts to dwindle away and you question your ability. I broke it back down to basics – trade smaller size, take simpler trades, no elaborate hedges (which at the time were not working for me). I even looked at a few different markets which I knew other traders had been finding profitable. It was a fine balance between banging my head against the wall trading the same way in the same markets causing my drawdown, or just searching for a holy grail somewhere else. I knew I'd never find it. Focus is a huge thing; concentrate; do the simple things well and build the confidence back up."
>
> **– A proprietary trader**

Within your trading process it is useful to think about what specific action you want to take

- following a losing trade

- during a period of drawdown

- after a mistake.

What is your process for dealing with difficult trading situations? Many traders give a lot of thought to the process of finding opportunities in the market, entering the market, managing the position and exiting the market. But little thought to the processes of dealing with challenging market and trading situations.

Actions to overcome challenges

Trading challenge, situation, event	Specific effective trading action to take

18

STAY CALM IN CRITICAL MOMENTS

COMPOSURE BUILDS CONFIDENCE

"To bear trials with a calm mind robs misfortune of its
strength and burden."

– Seneca

S AM TRADES A very illiquid product. There are times when he
has a plan for a trade and knows what he would like to do but is
simply unable to take the action he would like, thanks to a lack
of liquidity.

Understandably, this can be stressful.

Even more so if the market moves aggressively against him and he is
left simply observing his P&L dive deeper into the red. Large losses
combined with a lack of control are a sure-fire way to activate the
stress response.

In moments like this, the ability to manage your physiology – to be able to regulate your stress response – to maintain (or regain) a level of composure is important. It also enhances your confidence in being able to perform when the pressure is on.

In the trading moments that matter most – those that are the most stressful and demanding – it is *everything* that you have done in *all* of the moments leading up to that moment that will ultimately matter most.

There is no specific strategy or skill that can help you. You can't 'hack' your way out. What helps is your accumulation of training, experience and skill. The Navy SEALS have a saying that under stress you 'fall to your level of training'. No fancy trick can replace years of practice, experience and learning development.

In a moment of high pressure you can either confidently say 'I got this' or you can't. Elite performers are not faking it.

In more detail, it might be said to come down to:

1. experience

2. skill/competence

3. mindset

4. physiological state

5. preparation

6. state-management skills.

The first five of these six factors are developed and practised in advance of any stressful market moment occurring. The final one, *state management*, is an important skill that can help you to manage stress response in real time – and there are a variety of ways in which that can be achieved.

PUTTING THE BRAKES ON

When you experience a stress response, the body mobilises energy – preparing you for action. In your central nervous system the stress response activates through your sympathetic nervous system, essentially your body's 'accelerator'. Up to a certain level of activation, the energy in your system may be useful and useable – performance-enhancing.

There can be times, however, when the energy becomes too high. You are accelerating too fast – and your arousal level has a negative impact on your performance. In such situations you need to be able to put the brakes on. You need to be able to activate your parasympathetic nervous system: the body's braking system.

When it comes to regulating the activation of your central nervous system, the one key consciously controllable factor that can be utilised is *breathing*.

Parasympathetic and sympathetic nervous systems

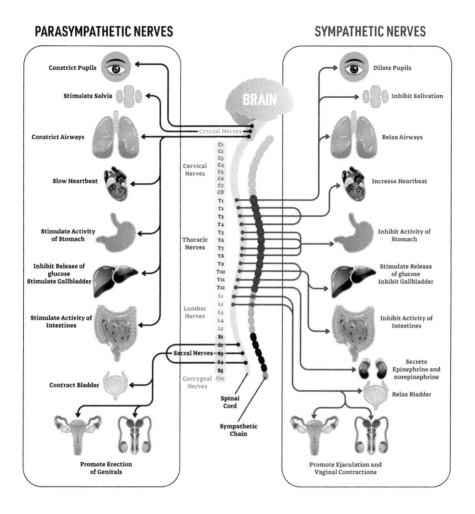

BREATHWORK

"The breathing strategies have been hugely helpful for me," was a piece of feedback I received from a PM at a large hedge fund following his participation in a series of performance-based workshops. It was echoed by everyone else in the group, including some highly experienced and successful PMs. "I have used them to help me achieve a calm focus while making trading decisions, and also to help with managing my stress levels when giving presentations to clients and to the media."

Your breath is with you in every moment – mostly outside your conscious awareness – shifting and changing in response to what is happening externally and internally. It reflects changes in your nervous system – speeding up with the activation of the sympathetic nervous system, and slowing down with the parasympathetic system. It shifts and changes as you ride the ups and downs of the markets, reflecting your brain's assessment of perceived levels of risk and reward (and as the brain activates emotions from fear to excitement, and mobilises energy for action).

There has been a growing interest in recent years in breathing practices and utilising breathing strategies to enhance people's health and performance. It has been a key part of my work with trading clients.

AWARENESS OF THE BREATH

A great starting point with *breathwork*, as it is known, is to simply begin to bring some awareness to your breath – to find some time to pay attention to how you are breathing.

Take a moment. Pause. Just observe your breath.

- What do you notice about the speed of your breathing?

- What do you notice about the depth of your breathing?

- What do you notice about the rhythm? The ratio of the in-breath to the out-breath?

- What do you notice about where you are breathing from? Are you breathing from the diaphragm (the belly area) or from the chest?

- What do you notice about what you are breathing through? Are you breathing through your mouth or your nose?

You could profitably spend a few minutes each day noticing your breath. No need to control anything. No need to do anything. Simply notice it. This is a very common mindfulness meditation-type practice.

BACK TO THE PRESENT

High performance often occurs *in the present moment.* And high levels of stress can pull people out of the present moment. Focus shifts from process to outcome; thinking shifts from 'what do I need to do in this moment?' to memories from the past or worries about the future.

One of the simplest and most effective techniques that I teach to my clients to help them bring a sense of calm or composure to a stressful moment is to simply take some slow mindful breaths – to take a few slower, deeper breaths with full awareness.

George Mumford, a mindfulness consultant to NBA teams in the USA, talks about how mindfulness can enable you to experience challenge and difficulty from within the "eye of the hurricane" – from the calm centre.[48] Taking a few slow, deep, mindful breaths can get you into the eye, and bring a sense of composure and calm to a challenging moment or situation in the markets.

TACTICAL BREATHING STRATEGIES

Elite sport and the military both utilise breathwork to enhance performance under pressure. Over recent years there has been an increasing interest in the science and application of utilising breathing strategies to enhance performance in high-stakes situations.

You probably think you are already good at breathing. You've had a lot of practice – a lifetime, in fact. You can do it without thinking. Of course, we can all breathe without thinking; it is an autonomic (automatic) function – it would be cumbersome and dangerous if it were otherwise.

However, while none of us were taught to breathe, and we are all basically competent at it, there are opportunities for us to enhance our breathing in general – for health and wellbeing, and to boost our performance, specifically under stress and pressure.

THE MECHANICS OF BREATHING

Before we get into some specific breathing strategies, I want to give you a few key pointers about the mechanics of breathing and how to enhance your breathing.

There are three key factors to consider when undertaking breathwork for performance enhancement:[49]

1. location

2. vessel

3. cadence.

1. Location

Take a moment. Bring attention to your breath. Observe *where* you are breathing from – the engine.

Is it the diaphragm – the belly (lower) – or is it the chest (higher)?

When people are in a stressed state, their breathing generally becomes faster, shallower and from the upper chest area. When people are more relaxed it is slower, deeper, from the diaphragm – belly – area.

Shifting your breathing from your chest to your belly is one way to engage the parasympathetic nervous system and put the brakes on.

2. Vessel

Take another moment. Bring attention to your breath. Observe what you are breathing *through*.

Is it your mouth or your nose?

Research into the science of breathing shows that *nasal breathing* is very powerful. When it comes to breathing strategies, especially those that have a focus on shifting stress physiology, it is more effective than mouth breathing.

We are designed to breathe through our noses. The nose has hair, sinuses and mucus all helping to filter air quality. When we breathe through the mouth this process is bypassed. The mouth is primarily a part of the digestive system. Only at very high levels of physical exertion should you need to use it to breathe.

Breathing through the nose also releases nitrogen oxide (NO), which sterilises the air you breathe, opens your airways (it is a bronchodilator) and helps improve oxygen uptake. Lastly, nasal breathing helps engage the diaphragm and is better at controlling how much oxygen we breathe in and how much carbon dioxide we breathe out. It is more efficient.

Inhale gently through your nose, pause, exhale gently through your nose, pause, repeat.

3. Cadence

Take a moment to pay attention to your breath: observe the rhythm of your breathing, how long the in-breath and the out-breath are in relation to each other.

The third factor in the mechanics of the breath is the cadence, the ratio of the length of the in-breath to the length of the out-breath. This determines the impact of your breathing on your physiological state.

When you breathe in, you activate the sympathetic nervous system, the accelerator, and when you breathe out you activate the parasympathetic nervous system, the brakes. Your in-breath puts energy into the system, your out-breath slows things down. By changing your cadence, the ratio between in- and out-breaths, you can change your physiological state.

- A '1:1' cadence has an equal length in-breath and out-breath. For example, breathe in for a count of four; breathe out for a count of four.

- A '1:2' cadence has an out-breath that is twice as long as the in-breath. For example, breathe in for a count of three; breathe out for a count of six.

- A '2:1' cadence has an in-breath that is twice as long as the out-breath. For example, breath in for a count of six; breathe out for a count of three.

THE ART OF BREATH

There are many different breathing techniques and strategies. Some traders prefer particular techniques to others. My advice is to try a variety. Experiment – away from the markets at first – and once you have found those that are most useful, you can begin to integrate them where appropriate within your trading.

Building five minutes a day of strategic breathwork into your trading process is a very effective way to develop your state-management skills and strengthen your physiology. The breathing techniques can then be used tactically in smaller doses, from a few seconds to a few minutes, throughout the trading day as required.

Calm and focused: The goal of this breathing technique is to balance your physiology. You want to be focused and engaged – but also calm. For this state, try a 1:1 cadence. In the military a 4:4 in-breath, out-breath pattern is often taught as **tactical breathing** for this. I have also used a **resonant** breathing pattern of 5:5 with many of my trading clients.

Calm and relaxed: The intention of this technique is to develop the ability to put the brakes on – to slow things down, to activate your body's relaxation response. To do this, a cadence of 1:2 is utilised. The out-breath is twice as long as the in-breath. Start with 3:6 – if this feels too uncomfortable, drop down to 2:4, then move back to 3:6 when it feels right. Over time, with practice, aim to get comfortable with 4:8.

19

DON'T BEAT YOURSELF UP

HARSH TRADING CRITIC OR COMPASSIONATE TRADING COACH?

"When I experienced my biggest ever trading losses, I realised how important my self-talk was. I had been reasonably consistent in the build-up to these hits – after them, I had no profits for the year to show. I had to work very hard to keep confidence in my ability to trade."

– A commodities trader

WHAT DO YOU say to yourself when you have lost money on a trade? Or when you are struggling during a tough period of drawdown? Or have made an execution error? Or missed out on a good trading opportunity?

I have heard some pretty brutal self-judgements from traders in my coaching sessions:

"You're a f****** idiot."

"You're a loser."

"You always mess things up."

And worse.

If you have ever beaten yourself up like this, firstly, you're normal. You may be surprised to hear that. The human mind has a tendency to judge and criticise, to find the negative, to predict the worst, to tell yourself stories about the future that invoke feelings of anxiety and fear – to become dissatisfied with what it has and to want more, and to dredge up painful memories from the past.

It is what minds do.

It is not abnormal, it is not wrong, but it may, of course, be profoundly unhelpful at times.

Being overly judgemental in your self-talk can impact your confidence and your trading performance. It is a tendency I have encountered in many high achievers across performance domains. Most people in general talk to themselves in ways that they would never dream of speaking to another person. In high achievers, the self-talk can be positively monstrous.

They often believe their harsh self-criticism drives them – that is a key to their success. But this is not necessarily true. It can be harmful, especially over the long term.

The keys to managing the impact of harsh self-judgement include:

- developing greater self-acceptance and self-compassion
- unhooking from your self-judgements
- engaging fully in effective trading action.

WHAT IS SELF-COMPASSION?

Compassion is not a word people instinctively mention when thinking about traders and trading – or in any other 'alpha'-type environment. However, growing research, particularly by Kristin Neff, demonstrates that *self-compassion* is an essential high-performance skill that builds emotional intelligence and resilience.[50]

Compassion is generally admired. It's demonstrated through behaviours such as kindness, sympathy and being supportive to others. Self-compassion involves acting in the same way *towards yourself* – when you are having a difficult time in your trading, when you are losing, when you make a mistake or notice something about yourself as a trader that you don't like.

Instead of defaulting to judgement and criticism, apply some self-compassion. Bring an understanding and appreciation of your situation, accept that you are human and fallible, that things will not always go your way. Be tolerant of the fact that you will lose money; you will make mistakes; you will miss trading opportunities; you will sometimes not follow your trading plan; you will fall short of your goals; you will get frustrated.

This is the trading experience. It is a reflection of the human condition.

THE THREE ELEMENTS OF SELF-COMPASSION

According to Neff's work, the three building blocks of self-compassion are:

1. Self-kindness (instead of self-judgement)

Self-kindness means being more accepting and understanding of yourself when things go wrong, instead of beating yourself up and being highly self-critical.

One of the keys to this is recognising that *imperfection is inevitable*. It is perfectly normal to experience failing, losing money, drawdown, making mistakes, missing opportunities, impatience, biases, urges and other difficulties within your trading.

Be less harsh on yourself when things are not going as you planned. Accept that you are human and fallible. Don't fight to be perfect. This reduces stress, frustration and self-criticism – and allows you to face your difficulties with greater equanimity.

2. Common humanity (instead of isolation)

Traders I work with in one-to-one coaching often feel that they're the only ones in the world suffering from their problem. It feels like they're the only trader out there who gets painfully angry or frustrated about losing money; or the only trader who feels ashamed about making a 'stupid' mistake; or the only trader who can't get past a deep sense of regret over not getting out of a losing trade.

Humans are imperfect and so therefore are traders. And all traders lose money, make mistakes, miss out on opportunities, fail to follow through on their trading plans, trade too small or too large, experience drawdown.

Part of self-compassion is about recognising that you are not experiencing these challenges in isolation. These challenges (and responses) are *shared across all traders*. They are part of the common trading experience.

3. Mindfulness (instead of over-identification)

Self-compassion involves taking a *balanced* approach to negative thoughts and feelings experienced in trading. This means that they are not supressed – but also not exaggerated.

The goal, as we discussed earlier in the book, is to be willing to be open to, accept and observe difficult thoughts and feelings, without trying to get rid of them. The aim is to be aware of your internal experience but not to get caught up in it and swept away reactively.

This is where developing your skills of present-moment attention and awareness, defusion/unhooking, and emotional acceptance plays a key role.

THE BENEFITS OF SELF-COMPASSION

People who have high levels of self-compassion are less judgemental about their own failures and mistakes. They recognise that failures, setbacks and difficult times are part of the human experience. And they are able to take a balanced approach to the negative thoughts and emotions that show up when experiencing a difficult time.

People with higher levels of self-compassion experience lower levels of psychological distress, less fear of failure, have greater motivation to recover after failure and setbacks, and are better at overcoming adversity.

Self-compassion as a trader is about recognising that failure and setbacks, tough times, and losses and mistakes are inevitable – but are also valuable learning opportunities. They're something to be accepted and approached, not avoided.

It is also about recognising your own areas of weakness and working on improving yourself in the context of becoming your best trading self.

WILL I LOSE MY COMPETITIVE EDGE IF I DEVELOP MY SELF-COMPASSION?

Many traders I have worked with have described themselves as being their 'own worst critic'. And many see this as valuable. They say their self-criticism drives them to keep trading and improving, to learn from their losses and mistakes.

But being highly self-critical can undermine your faith in yourself. It can:

- reduce your desire to take on new tasks

- increase the risk of anxiety and depression

- lower your self-efficacy

- increase fear of failure

- inhibit goal achievement

- reduce self-awareness

- hinder working on areas of weakness.

Many traders worry that unless they are being hard on themselves, they will lose their competitive edge. But this is not the case.

Developing self-compassion towards trading difficulties enables you to learn from and overcome challenges you face – without the negative effects of being harshly self-critical. Some suggest that self-compassion is a more adaptive approach to failure than self-criticism because it requires greater effort – and prompts greater motivation – to improve.

PRACTISING SELF-COMPASSION, ENHANCING CONFIDENCE

There are many ways you can develop self-compassion. It is a skill. And like any skill, it can be practised.

One of the quickest and simplest is to create an intention to *talk to yourself like you would talk to a valued friend or colleague*. Do this all the time. But especially when you experience a tough time in your trading.

Consider how a supportive coach would help you through a difficult situation or period.

1. Think about times when a trader you know might feel bad about themselves. How would you respond? Write down what you would say and do. Note the tone of your words.

2. Now think about times when you feel bad about yourself. How do you typically respond to yourself in these situations? Write down what you typically do and say to yourself. Note the tone in which you talk to yourself.

3. Is there a difference? If so, in what ways? Why might this be? What factors lead you to treat yourself and others so differently?

4. Write down how you think things might change if you responded to yourself in the same way you typically respond to another trader when struggling and having a tough time.

Being aware of your self-talk, and unhooking from harsh-self judgements, is also highly beneficial. This involves the process of defusion we covered in chapter 15. Take time to label your critical thoughts as 'judging' – observe them as judgements from your mind. 'These are thoughts I am thinking...' This helps take the sting out of them, revealing them for what they are – mental events of no particular infallibility or finality.

Another practice you can use is to add another section to your trading journal, where you spend five minutes at the end of the day writing about a difficult situation you experienced where you were harshly critical and judgemental about yourself. Note down how you felt and why. As in chapter 16, this helps you get past these unhelpful thoughts through defusion, processing and reflection.

One last practice is to think about situations where you are typically harsh on yourself. Write down the exact words that you say to yourself in those situations and how they make you feel. Then take the perspective of a compassionate trading coach, who has your best interests at heart, who supports you and wants you to achieve your trading potential. Write down what they might say in that same situation, and the impact that it would have on you.

Situation	Self-talk	Feelings	Coach's words	Impact

PART
EIGHT

FLEXIBILITY

20

FIND THE OPPORTUNITY IN THE DIFFICULT

NEGATIVITY BIAS

You are shown pictures of a Ferrari, a dead cat and a plate.

How would you feel about each one?

At the same time, your brain's electrical activity – specifically in the cerebral cortex, where information processing occurs – is recorded. What would you expect to happen?

This was some research conducted by John Cacioppo PhD looking at how our brain reacts to different stimuli.[51]

Participants were shown:

- a Ferrari (known to arouse positive feelings)

- a dead cat (negative feelings)

- a plate (neutral).

The research demonstrated that the brain reacts more strongly to negative stimuli. There is greater electrical activity – negative outweighs positive.

We have, in other words, a negativity bias. Our brain is simply more sensitive to negative events. This is key to our survival. It keeps us out of harm's way. Being attentive to threats has been valuable since the beginning of time.

And when we are under stress, this bias is amplified. We become hypervigilant to threat and risk, much more focused on the negative. This can be unhelpful in making effective trading decisions. It is important to balance this negativity bias out.

One effective way is to shift your perspective. The skill of *flexible perspective-taking* is one of the keys to avoiding your natural psychological reactions trapping you.

FINDING THE OPPORTUNITY

opportunitiesarenowhere

What can you see in the above?

Some of you will have seen opportunities are *nowhere*.

Some of you will have seen opportunities are *now here*.

We all had the same letters in the same order, yet there are two different messages that might be perceived within.

What would the experience be of a trader who approaches the markets through the lens of *opportunities are nowhere*?

And what would the experience be of a trader who approaches the market through the lens of *opportunities are now here*?

How you view the markets has an impact on how you feel and behave, and the decisions that you make. This in turn effects what you get out of the markets.

I have encountered many traders who have an *opportunities are nowhere* mindset. Not long after the Global Financial Crisis one trader told me that "trading is over". The results of this are not productive.

A bulletproof trader needs the ability to find the opportunity within the difficult. Negativity bias makes it easy to adopt the *opportunities are nowhere* mindset; commitment and practice are required to retrain the brain to achieve balance with an *opportunities are now here* perspective.

I sometimes refer to this perspective as *taking a wide lens*. It is about being mentally flexible. And it promotes the taking of effective trading action.

"During difficult periods come the best opportunities."
– A fund manager

Some useful questions to help find the opportunity in difficult times include:

- What is the opportunity in this situation?
- What is good about this situation?
- What could I learn from this situation?
- What skills or knowledge can I develop in this situation?
- How could this experience make me a better trader?
- What could I learn or gain from this experience?

Often difficult situations, challenging times and obstacles are ultimately valuable for traders. They prove to be developmental – hidden opportunities and valuable lessons. The skill is finding the opportunity and leveraging it. The Stoics always aimed to get the best out of every situation, even loss and tragedy. They would try to find the lessons to be learned – *and the meaningful action to be taken as a result.*

Paradoxically, it is only by facing and overcoming challenges and difficulties that you can develop the psychological skills you need to achieve your full potential as a trader, including:

- commitment
- confidence
- resilience
- flexibility
- composure.

LEARNING VS EARNING

"A good person dyes events with his own colour and turns whatever happens to his own benefit."

– Seneca

In one of my long-term consulting contracts with a global trading company, I worked with a number traders who for one reason or another were encountering a sustained period of losses or reduced profitability. These periods were always psychologically difficult. It was tough for the traders to get through them. While I utilised a variety of approaches and strategies for each trader – based on their own unique situations, experience levels, trading styles and markets, personalities and preferences – there was one framework I found myself utilising regularly.

It was a mental shift; a change of perspective *from earning to learning*.

When traders are performing well and making money, my experience is that their focus is fully on earning. It's all about P&L maximisation.

Very few attempt to develop their skills, knowledge or strategies. The opportunity is maximising profits, 'making hay while the sun shines' in farming parlance.

Only when traders are faced with losses, drawdown and changes in market dynamics do they tend to become highly reflective. That's when they get introspective – and open to the possibility of developing new skills or knowledge. This is a learning-focused phase – the opportunity is skill and knowledge development. Honing the craft, mind and body. Flexing or adapting their strategies and trading behaviour.

In the diagram below we can see how, after a period of good returns, there can often be periods of lower returns. And these periods of lower returns can be followed by periods of higher returns. Trading performance is cyclical. This is often a reflection of changes in market conditions, and the synchronicity between market dynamics and a trader's style and strategies.

The danger for traders going through this cycle is that, as a result of the discomfort of the down cycle and attempts to avoid it, they end up engaging in destructive behaviours. Such as:

- failing to adapt their approach

- taking excessive risk

- trading markets they are not skilled at.

All in order to make money; to earn. In these down cycles it is important to recognise the shift in conditions. And at that point you should make a mindset shift: from earning to learning.

This leads to engaging in different, more helpful behaviours – actions relevant to the new context. These are what ultimately get you out of the down cycle more effectively.

The skills, knowledge and behaviours practised and developed during one down cycle become resources to get through the next one. They may also add value, enabling higher P&L in future earning cycles.

The earning–learning cycle

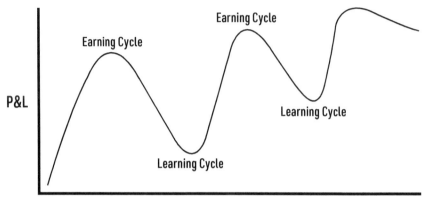

THE OPPORTUNITY TO GET COMFORTABLE WITH THE UNCOMFORTABLE

There is always one opportunity that exists during difficult trading times. That is, of course, the opportunity to get better at trading during difficult times.

You get good at dealing with losses when you are losing. You get good at dealing with drawdown when you are in drawdown. You get good at adapting your trading style to changing market conditions when the markets are changing. The skills of dealing with the difficult are forged when it is difficult. Every tough trading experience is an opportunity to practise and forge your inner citadel, to build your inner fortress and become more bulletproof.

Adversity is part of the trading experience. It is an opportunity to gain physiological exposure and adaptive toughness, and to gain psychological exposure and the development of your mental and emotional skills and resources.

Difficult times are uncomfortable. They are therefore great opportunities to practise getting comfortable with the uncomfortable

– to learn to be willing to accept the difficult, and to practise taking committed action. To develop your poise.

THE VIEW FROM ABOVE

The Stoics had a practice of viewing the world from above. It was about neutrally observing the comings and goings of the world, and your experience within it, rather than being caught up in it.

Viewing the world from above does not change what is happening in the world. But a different perspective *does* change how you experience what is happening. Viewing the world from above allows you take a different perspective on your trading experience. When times are tough it is easy to get caught up in the short term, the here and now. To get hooked by your thoughts, wrapped up in your feelings. It can feel intense and uncomfortable.

A losing trade seen from above can be put into perspective, set among *all* the trades you have ever taken; it is one of many. A period of drawdown viewed from above allows you to experience it with less attachment to the thoughts and emotions that come with it. You can have a more neutral perspective, be better able to see the opportunities that lie within, and make more effective choices for action.

"Take a view from above – look at the thousands of flocks and herds, the thousands of human ceremonies, every sort of voyage in storm or calm, the range of creation, combination, and extinction. Consider, too, the lives once lived by others long before you, the lives that will be lived after you, the lives lived now among foreign tribes; and how many have never even heard your name, how many will soon forget it, how many may praise you now but quickly turn to blame. Reflect that neither memory nor fame, nor anything else at all, has any importance worth thinking of."[52]

– Marcus Aurelius

Here is a practice you can utilise to help get a different perspective on a trading challenge.

> Sit in a comfortable place and close your eyes.
>
> Now use your imagination: picture yourself at your desk from above.
>
> As you look at yourself, rise up, pull back, and notice your location, your building, the town, the world.
>
> Put your trading challenge in relation to what you are seeing at each stage as you rise above.
>
> Notice also that there are many other traders confronting challenges in their trading.

WHAT WOULD A ROLE MODEL DO?

Think of a difficult or stressful situation in your trading.

Now think about a trading role model you have. Maybe someone you know, or know of, or have read about; maybe even an imaginary 'ideal trader'.

What would your trading role model or ideal self do in this difficult situation?

In a difficult trading moment, bringing the question of 'What would my role model do?' can allow you to create a pause between stimulus and response, reduce reactivity and bring a different perspective to a situation. And it can enable you to decide upon the best possible response.

The Stoics called this practice 'contemplating the sage', and would ask 'What would the sage do?' in times of challenge and difficulty.

" 'We need to set our affections on some good man and keep him constantly before our eyes, so that we may live as if he were watching us and do everything as if he saw what we were doing.' This was Epicurus's advice, and in giving it he has given us a guardian and moral tutor – and not without reason, either: misdeeds are greatly diminished if a witness is always standing near intending doers."

– Seneca

21

GET GOOD AT
ADAPTING TO CHANGE

CHANGE IS INEVITABLE

"Cling tooth and nail to the following rule: Not to give in to adversity,
never to trust prosperity, and always to take full note of Fortune's habit
of behaving just as she pleases, treating her as if she were actually
going to do everything it is in her power to do. Whatever you have been
expecting for some time comes as less of a shock."

– Seneca

CHANGE IS INEVITABLE – it is probably one of the few certainties in trading. The Stoics believed that everything needs to change so that new things could evolve in life. They considered people who were surprised by change to be foolish. How could you not know change was coming? Seneca advises not to give in to adversity, that bad times do not last forever, and also to recognise that good times do not last forever – everything is impermanent.

FLOORED: SURVIVAL OF THE MOST ADAPTABLE

"In 1997, 10,000 people traded on the floors...
Today, about 10% remain."

This is the opening to the 2009 documentary *Floored*, which tells the story of the closing of the trading pits in Chicago as electronic trading arrived.[53] It follows some of the traders who worked there and their attempts to adapt to the new world of trading.

One of my favourite scenes – and one that I often show in my workshops – has floor trader Kenny Ford having a discussion with ex-floor trader Mike Fishbain, now a software engineer. They talk about the evolution of the markets, the rise of the machine – and how terrible electronic trading is.

It's a great example of someone who can see change happening, does not like it, and does not want to change either.

Some of Kenny's perspectives include:

"The computer is the most evil thing ever invented"

"I can't beat the computer"

"Open outcry is the most honourable way of trading ever invented"

"Believe me when I say they are cheating on the machines"

My favourite response from an exasperated Mike is:

"Imagine you are a musician. You like playing jazz, but it doesn't mean you can't play classical. You prefer the jazz, but you can still play the classical. The market is like a symphony. You have to play the music that you are given."

In a world where change is a constant, *Floored* shows the reality of what happens when traders are faced with serious shifts in the trading world. In basic evolutionary terms, some traders survive and some die. To use the words attributed to Charles Darwin:

> "It is not the strongest of the species that survives, nor the most intelligent that survives. It is the one that is most adaptable to change."

SURVIVAL IS NOT MANDATORY

If you'd had a heart attack and were told you had to change your lifestyle to avoid a second heart attack (and, potentially, death), what would you do?

I am guessing you would say you'd make the changes required – eat more healthily, exercise more frequently. Who wouldn't when faced with a choice between *change or die?*

But the reality is that most people don't. It seems incredible – what better motivator could there be than taking effective action or death? But roughly nine out of ten people do not make the changes they need to in such situations.[54] Many end up dying.

When I first started working with traders in 2005 it was at a large global proprietary trading group in London. In the first few months it became evident that many of the more senior traders were struggling to generate the returns they desired – not due to a lack of trading skill or knowledge, but simply because the markets had become more efficient.

The edge they once had was no longer there.

What they were doing on a daily basis was not working. Some of those traders made a significant effort to adapt their trading styles and strategies, struggled through and persevered – and sustained their trading careers. Others kept doing what they had always done. It kept not working. And eventually the stress of continually not making money, and the losses they incurred, led to them leaving.

Over my time coaching traders since then, I have seen over and over again how the ability to adapt to changing markets is one of the most important characteristics for sustained high performance. Any edge a trader has in the market is temporary. The ability to both flex in the short term and to adapt in the long term are pre-requisites for both P&L maximisation and market longevity.

Ultimately, whether traders choose to change or not is down to them. In the words of W. Edwards Deming: "It is not necessary to change. Survival is not mandatory."

THE FUTURES LAB

One successful trader I worked with spent a proportion of his time thinking about what might be coming up in the markets and in trading. His goal was to look for potential shifts and opportunities that could occur in future. He would prepare for them *now*, putting him at the front of the adaptation curve should anything happen.

In a way it was a process of research and development. He was prepared for performance in the future, all the while maintaining performance in the short term.

This process of looking forward and developing plans and strategies for the future has been a key approach of UK Sport in its goal of winning as many Olympic medals as possible. For instance, they asked:

- What will be the future global trends and megatrends in 2024 that will shape the world of elite sport?
- Where will be the limits of athletic performance?

- How will we be managing athlete health?

- How will our successful leaders and coaches operate?

- How will our industry be interfacing with technology and big data?

- GB succeeded in doing what no one thought possible at the Rio Olympics and beat China. Is it conceivable that they can take on the USA – and how?

- Which emerging technologies have the potential to revolutionise athletes' training and performance, and how?

- How could the UK's high-performance system reduce its reliance on public sector funding? What are the alternative business models?

- Where are the future GB medallists no one has spotted?

These are all questions from UK Sports Futures Lab, where a diverse range of experts from a variety of different academic, practical, business and sporting backgrounds gather for a day several times a year.[55] They think carefully about the future of sport and what the elite performance world will look like in four to eight years' time. It's an attempt to develop athletes in various Olympic sports to perform at their best in future. Discussions are had; ideas generated; questions asked.

The result is action, including funding and support to develop new technology, training processes, and anything else that might give athletes and teams an edge over their competition.

I often use a similar process with my clients. It's a pragmatic and powerful way of getting traders and trading teams to think about the future, to look at where the world of trading is heading, and to consider gaining new knowledge, skills and strategies in advance. To be proactive rather than reactive.

- What does the future of trading look like for you?

- What five issues would be useful to consider?

- Who do you need to become to trade well in the future environment?

- What will be the same?

- What will you need to start doing or do more of?

- What will you need to stop doing or do less of?

ADAPTING TO NEW MARKETS EFFECTIVELY

Adapting to new markets is essentially a process of change. Some traders find change easier than others. Some embrace it, others are more cautious. Being able to survive over the long term in the markets requires traders to adapt.

Below are seven factors that influence how successfully traders adapt to trading new markets. You can harness them in your own adaptation process.

1. RECOGNISING

The first step is having an awareness that the markets are changing, that how you are trading currently may not be sustainable for the future.

One of the challenges that traders face with adapting to changing markets is assessing whether the markets are in a short-term change or making a longer-term more systemic shift. My own perspective is that, where traders are in a state of continual assessment and evaluation of their own trading, this becomes a little more obvious. But it is ultimately a judgement call in an environment categorised by uncertainty, novelty and uncontrollability.

2. READINESS

There is a difference between recognising that the markets are changing and actually making the changes you need to make as a result. I have worked with many traders who have seen the markets changing, yet are not committed to making the changes required of them.

When I am working with clients I am assessing where they are in terms of readiness to change. If they are not prepared to change, there is often little I can do for them at that time. We can't really work together until they are ready. *'When the student is ready the teacher appears.'*

3. REFRAME

People typically see change as a threat. A negative. When traders have to adapt to new markets, they are typically giving up an edge and looking for a new one. Profitability will be reduced. Time and effort must be invested in developing new skills, knowledge and strategy with little short-term monetary gain.

Essentially there needs to be a shift in mindset from an 'earning' focused one to a 'learning' focused one. It is often only in cases of challenge and difficulty, such as changing market conditions, that traders commit to learning and developing new skills and knowledge. When times are good the mandate is to just keep trading and earning money.

Ask yourself:

- What could be good about this change?
- What could I learn?
- How could it develop my trading/make me a better trader?

4. RELATIONSHIP

Having people support you as you adapt your trading can be extremely helpful. It has been shown to be one of the key factors of successful change programmes; having a coach/facilitator or a peer group (or both) providing support to help keep people on track, share concerns, and to provide encouragement makes a crucial difference. This role is core to my work as a coach to traders going through tough times.

- Who can support you when making changes to your trading?

5. REPETITION

Ultimately change is about taking action, about doing things differently. The key is to identify the specific steps that you need to take – researching new markets, experimenting with new trading strategies, acquiring relevant knowledge, developing new skills, etc.

- Why is making this change important to you?
- What value, strength or action quality can you leverage?
- What specific actions do you need to take?

6. RESISTANCE

During the process of changing and adapting it is highly likely that difficult thoughts and emotions show up. This is perfectly normal. Fear, frustration, anxiety and thoughts such as 'This isn't working', 'This is taking too long', 'I'm not making enough P&L', may arise. This is where having the skills to work with your thoughts and emotions becomes critical, allowing you to stay focused on taking the action that is important to you: committed action.

7. RELAPSE

"I tried it and it didn't work" is a typical phrase I hear when working with traders adapting to new markets.

"What did you do?" I ask.

"I have gone back to my old way of trading."

The process of making a change is not linear *or* exponential. It is more like an uptrend. There are periods of upward momentum – and then a pullback; or, in psychological terms, a relapse.

Relapse is normal in a change process. It is what you do when you relapse that determines whether you change or not. Many people interpret relapse as failure and go back to their old ways. When people are aware that relapse is a part of the change process they can prepare for it, and respond to it differently, by recognising it as relapse, resetting and going again, driving the next period of upward momentum.

Relapse in the change process is like a pull back in the market

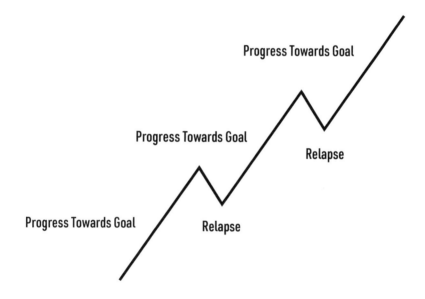

PART NINE

STATE MANAGEMENT

22

MONITOR YOUR STRESS AND FATIGUE LEVELS

THE PHYSIOLOGY OF TRADING PERFORMANCE

C AN YOU THINK of a time in your trading when you were aware that your stress level was high? What was the impact on your trading behaviour and decision-making?

How about a time in your trading when you felt tired, fatigued, maybe even exhausted? What was the impact on your trading behaviour and decision-making?

How you feel physiologically has a huge impact on your psychological functioning. It profoundly influences:

- your levels of focus and awareness

- the quality of your thinking

- the emotions you experience

- your impulsivity

- the risks you take

- the decisions you make.

Your brain is embodied. That is, it sits within your body. It is deeply connected to it. There is no real mind/body split. As such, your physiological state – how stressed and fatigued you are – plays a significant role in how your brain functions, and in your risk-taking and decision-making as a trader.

FATIGUE MAKES COWARDS OF US ALL

In a study that looked at 1,100 parole decisions over a 12-month period, there was one variable that the researchers found dramatically affected the probability of being paroled: time of day.[56]

Prisoners who appeared early in the morning received parole about 70% of the time. Those who appeared late in the day were paroled less than 10% of the time.

Making decisions is energy dependent. When fatigue sets in, the brain has to make decisions with fewer resources – so it defaults to a neurological state known as *cognitive ease*. This involves a mandate of making quicker and easier decisions, using mental shortcuts where possible. For a fatiguing parole board, the simplest, quickest and lowest-risk choice is to keep prisoners incarcerated.

A summary of the impact of fatigue on decision-making reveals several key consequences:

- the adoption of low-effort strategies

- reduced high-level thinking and greater risk of bias

- quicker, less well-thought-out decisions

- impaired risk perception

- weighting of decision towards minimum effort for action

- reduced self-control

- increased risk of error.

In the longer term, fatigue has an impact on your health and on levels of commitment and motivation. It also leads to a bias towards risk aversion. As famous American football coach Vince Lombardi once stated: "Fatigue makes cowards of us all."

STRESS-INDUCED IRRATIONAL PESSIMISM

Short-term, acute stress – such as a sharp move in the market, increased volatility, your position going offside, a losing trade, making an error – can activate your stress response. If extreme enough, it can lead to a reduction in cognitive capacity, impacting your decision-making capability.

When stress extends over a *prolonged* period of time, you can experience a range of highly detrimental effects. An extended losing run, or a period of continuous change in the markets, or an excessive challenge can result in you experiencing what is called *chronic stress*.

This longer-term exposure leads to a state often described as *irrational pessimism*, underpinned by high levels of cortisol within the body. Traders become hypersensitive to threat and risk in the present, selectively recalling threatening episodes from the past and projecting danger ahead in the future.

As a result, traders become risk averse. At the extreme, they experience symptoms of depression, exhaustion and numbness – like being 'stuck on low'. (At the other end of things, they can become 'stuck on high' – with insomnia, hyper-arousal and feelings of agitation and restlessness.)

Stress is a high-energy state. It has a metabolic (energy) demand. The greater the stress and the more it is prolonged, the greater the energy costs – and the greater the risk of fatigue in the short term and burnout in the long.

Managing your levels of stress and fatigue is key to optimising your physiology so that you can make your best trading decisions. It also helps you be more robust at coping with demands and challenges. A strong physiology is a resilient physiology.

Two important skills are required for managing and developing your physiology effectively:

1. physiological state monitoring

2. physiological state management.

1.PHYSIOLOGICAL STATE MONITORING

It has been said that if you take a frog and throw it into a pan of boiling water it will immediately attempt to jump out – an example of an acute, short-term stress event akin to a big market move.

But if you put the frog into a pan of cold water and very slowly turn up the heat, it can end up boiling alive. This is similar to chronic stress, a slower, more gradual experience, like that of a sustained losing run.

I have worked with many traders going through stressful and difficult periods in their trading. In a significant number of cases there has been one notable similarity – they sought help towards the low point of their experience, *having already endured a long period of struggle and difficulty.*

In many cases, traders only seek help when they have reached a profoundly uncomfortable moment. They reach out when stress or fatigue is almost unendurable, and results have been consistently horrendous. But at this point, like the frog, they are already boiling – or close to.

In many of these cases the downtrend in their P&L, psychology and physiology would have been visible well before this low. Recovering from such low points often requires significant time and effort. And it means starting from a point where psychological and physiological capacities are reduced.

So it is incredibly helpful for traders to notice such changes *earlier* – and also, of course, to have the skills to act on the warning signs effectively.

Traders need to be aware of their physiological state not just over time, but also in the moment, and have the tools over both time frames to manage their state, so that they can trade at their best.

2.PHYSIOLOGICAL STATE MANAGEMENT

The core focus of physiological awareness is being aware of what is going on in your body. How stressed are you? How fatigued? One way this awareness can be developed is through subjective assessment such as tracking how well you have slept, your perceived stress and energy levels, and your mood and motivation on a 1–10 scaling basis.

David was a market maker at a bank who I met while providing coaching for his trading desk. He was very successful, very consistent and very well regarded by the rest of his desk. The area he chose to work on in his coaching was his *emotional reactivity* to specific trading events. I asked him to record, for every hour from waking till going to bed:

- his energy level on a scale of 1–10

- his stress level on a scale of 1–10

- and to write down the dominant emotion he was feeling at the time.

By tracking his stress level, energy level and emotional state he brought an increased awareness to them in the moment. He was able to notice the shifting of his physiological state through the day and in response to events. And he was able to reflect back on them and look at events from the trading day against his *internal experience*.

One of the interesting insights he had was in relation to what he termed the *stress–energy spread*; as stress increased and energy declined – as the spread widened – so his reactivity increased. Monitoring this spread provided a useful level of awareness for him. Importantly, the 'data' and the insights gained allowed us to develop a number of tactical self-management techniques that proved very helpful.

Subjective self-monitoring strategies like this can be effective. However, it is also now possible to get objective insights into a trader's physiology, stress and fatigue levels. This is thanks to the development of physiological measuring and assessment technology.

OBJECTIVE PHYSIOLOGICAL FEEDBACK

Over the last few years I have spent an increasing amount of time helping traders to monitor and manage their physiological states. A key tool in this has been the use of technology that provides objective insights into their stress, sleep, recovery and physical activity and fitness levels.

In my experience, the majority of traders like data. They're fans of charts and graphs. And they favour objectivity over subjectivity where possible.

Almost every trader I have worked with understands that they trade better when they are less stressed and fatigued, and that managing stress, getting good sleep, eating well and being physically active are all key components of trading well. But for all of us there is a gap between the knowing and the doing. Objective, data-driven assessment and monitoring can therefore much more deeply engage traders in the impact of their physiology on their trading – and this leads to greater adherence to the behaviours needed to enhance that physiology.

In my own work I have utilised a physiological marker known as *heart rate variability* (HRV), a derivative of heart rate (HR). This offers interesting insights into the functioning of the autonomic nervous system, the sympathetic (stress) and parasympathetic (recovery) systems.

When your heart beats there is a gap between consecutive beats. These gaps vary in length: this varying time interval is your heart rate variability (see diagram). HRV varies a lot between individuals. It is influenced by genetics (about 30%), age, health and fitness levels.

In general, a high HRV (meaning a greater variability of time intervals between heartbeats) is indicative of good fitness and health, and a stronger physiological state. Meanwhile, low HRV (less variability between time intervals of heartbeats) is associated with lower health and fitness, a weaker physiological state.

Heart rate variability – R-R Intervals

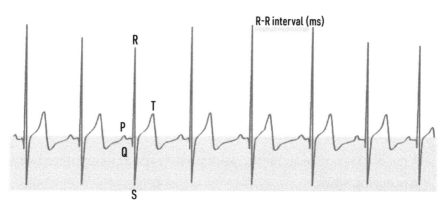

Source: Firstbeat

By asking traders to wear high-tech monitors – such as those used by elite athletes and sports teams – for a number of consecutive trading days, and by taking morning HRV readings, I have been able to objectively observe the impact of a trader's experience in the markets on their physiology – and, of course, vice versa.

From these observations I been able to test how making changes to a trader's lifestyle habits – sleep, recovery, physical activity and alcohol consumption – and the use of mental training strategies such as mindfulness meditation, breathing strategies and relaxation techniques can impact their HRV number.

WHO WOULD YOU GIVE YOUR CAPITAL TO?

Below are physiological profiles for two different traders. Each represents a 24-hour period.

The red (or darkest) bars indicate a stress response which can be positive or negative, the green (or medium grey) bars recovery, and the blue (pale grey) bars physical activity and movement. The higher the bars, the higher the response.

Here are some questions to consider:

- What do you notice about the number of stress bars during the day?

- What do you notice about the number of recovery bars during the sleep period?

- What do you notice about the amount of stress reactions and the amount of recovery?

- What do you notice about the amount of recovery in the daytime?

- What do you notice about the work periods and amount of recovery bars during work?

- What do you notice about the sleep, quantity and recovery?

TRADER A

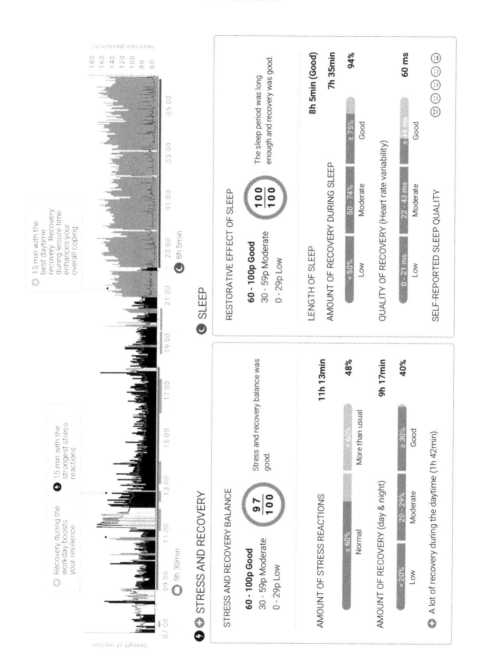

SLEEP

RESTORATIVE EFFECT OF SLEEP — 100/100

The sleep period was long enough and recovery was good.

60 - 100p Good
30 - 59p Moderate
0 - 29p Low

LENGTH OF SLEEP — 8h 5min (Good)

AMOUNT OF RECOVERY DURING SLEEP — 7h 35min

< 50% Low | 50 - 74% Moderate | ≥ 75% Good — 94%

QUALITY OF RECOVERY (Heart rate variability)

0 - 21 ms Low | 22 - 43 ms Moderate | ≥ 44 ms Good — 60 ms

SELF-REPORTED SLEEP QUALITY

STRESS AND RECOVERY

STRESS AND RECOVERY BALANCE — 97/100

Stress and recovery balance was good.

60 - 100p Good
30 - 59p Moderate
0 - 29p Low

AMOUNT OF STRESS REACTIONS — 11h 13min

≤ 60% Normal | > 60% More than usual — 48%

AMOUNT OF RECOVERY (day & night) — 9h 17min

< 20% Low | 20 - 29% Moderate | ≥ 30% Good — 40%

A lot of recovery during the daytime (1h 42min).

15 min with the best daytime recovery. Recovery during leisure time enhances your overall coping.

8h 5min

15 min with the strongest stress reactions

Recovery during the workday boosts your resilience

9h 30min

Heart rate (beats/min)
180 160 140 120 100 80 60

Strength of reaction

07.00 09.00 11.00 13.00 15.00 17.00 19.00 21.00 23.00 01.00 03.00 05.00

TRADER B

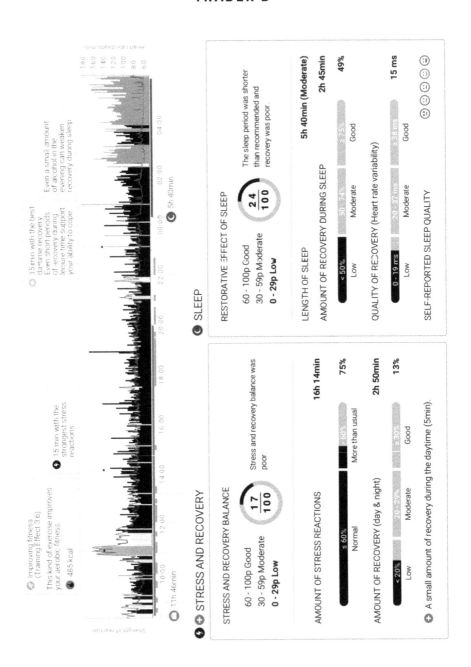

○ Improving fitness
(Training Effect 3.6)
This kind of exercise improves
your aerobic fitness.
● 485 kcal

○ 15 min with the best
daytime recovery
Even short periods
of recovery during
leisure time support
your ability to cope

○ 15 min with the best
daytime recovery
Even short periods
of recovery during
leisure time support
your ability to cope

○ Even a small amount
of alcohol in the
evening can weaken
recovery during sleep

● 15 min with the
strongest stress
reactions

○ 11h 46min   ● 5h 40min

☾ **SLEEP**

RESTORATIVE EFFECT OF SLEEP $\frac{24}{100}$

60 - 100p Good
30 - 59p Moderate
0 - 29p Low

The sleep period was shorter
than recommended and
recovery was poor.

LENGTH OF SLEEP   **5h 40min (Moderate)**

AMOUNT OF RECOVERY DURING SLEEP   **2h 45min**

< 50%	50-74%	≥ 75%	49%
Low	Moderate	Good	

QUALITY OF RECOVERY (Heart rate variability)

0 - 19 ms	20-37 ms	≥ 38 ms	15 ms
Low	Moderate	Good	

SELF-REPORTED SLEEP QUALITY   ☺ ☺ ☺ ☺ ☺

STRESS AND RECOVERY

STRESS AND RECOVERY BALANCE $\frac{17}{100}$

60 - 100p Good
30 - 59p Moderate
0 - 29p Low

Stress and recovery balance was
poor.

AMOUNT OF STRESS REACTIONS   **16h 14min**

≤ 60%	> 60%	75%
Normal	More than usual	

AMOUNT OF RECOVERY (day & night)   **2h 50min**

<20%	20-29%	≥30%	13%
Low	Moderate	Good	

○ A small amount of recovery during the daytime (5min).

206

Without going into detailed explanations of the data, but with a general understanding that these charts reflect a trader's physiology – that red (or the darkest shade in the print book) is stress, green (medium grey) is recovery and blue (very pale grey) is physical activity – you can probably begin to make some interesting observations.

Trader B has a few key physiological points of interest:

- 75% of his 24-hour day is spent in stress; only 13% in recovery – the recommended guidelines are 30%. Both fall outside the norm.

- He spends 11 hours and 46 minutes working, with no recovery.

- His sleep is 5 hours 40 minutes, and the amount of recovery and quality of recovery is low.

- He does get a 34-minute dose of physical activity in, which is health-promoting.

Looking at Trader A's data:

- 48% of his 24-hour day is in stress; 40% in recovery.

- He has a 9.5-hour working day, with 30 minutes of recovery.

- His sleep is 8 hours and 5 minutes, and the amount and quality of recovery are good.

- He gets a 27-minute dose of physical activity in, which is health promoting.

Imagine that these 24-hour periods are representative of a standard day for these traders. (Which, based on my longer samples, they were.) What would be the impact on stress and fatigue levels? What would be the physiological level of functioning? How would this impact how they felt and thought? How would this impact their risk-taking, decision-making and performance?

If you were given the choice of allocating your own capital to one or the other – assuming that their skills, knowledge, and strategy returns were relatively equal – who would you give your capital to?

STATE MANAGEMENT

The benefit of state-monitoring practices is developing state awareness and enabling self-management. This opens up preventative and in-the-moment state-management strategies that help you optimise and regulate your physiology to trade at your best.

By regularly monitoring your physiology you can gain insights into the impact that your experience of trading the markets has on it – and vice versa.

Several factors influence your HRV and are under your control. They can be approached as a part of your trading routine, or used tactically as required. Including:

- physical health and wellbeing
- sleep
- recovery
- physical fitness
- nutrition
- breathwork
- meditation
- biofeedback.

There are some key ways in which you can monitor you physiological state:

Subjective

Decide upon some physiological factors to monitor. Keep a record of these on a daily basis – or, if helpful, throughout the day. Ones I typically have clients record are:

- stress levels

- energy levels

- sleep

- mood

- emotional state.

These can all be recorded on a 1–5 or 1–10 scale in your journal or in a spreadsheet.

Objective

- Wearable technology – there has been a big increase in the quantity and quality of wearable technology that captures physiological data on your stress levels, sleep quality/ quantity, physical activity levels and fitness. The reliability of these does vary. But even those that are inacurrate will be consistently inaccurate, allowing for trends and patterns to be observed. These are a good and relatively affordable way to start collecting 24/7 data on your physiology.

- Daily HRV monitoring – there are a range of apps available which allow you to capture a daily HRV reading (readings can also be conducted through the day). You can then add some subjective input for tracking key physiological variables. This is a quick and simple way to track your physiological trends, and to gain insights into what lifestyle and work factors are affecting your HRV number and your physiological state. To get accurate readings invest in a high-quality heart-rate monitor to use with the appropriate app.

- Three-day performance lifestyle assessment – this is a more in-depth, accurate and costly approach to assessing your physiological state, including stress quantity and quality, sleep quality and quantity, physical activity levels and VO2 max fitness levels. It requires wearing a heart-based monitor with electrodes for a 72-hour period, at the end of which a detailed report is produced and feedback is given. The examples of traders' physiological data that I have used in this book have come from this type of assessment.

In the next two chapters I will be providing strategies to train and manage your physiological state, to develop high-performance lifestyle factors, and to build a high level of physiological fitness.

23

MASTER THE ART OF RECOVERY

ADAPTIVE TOUGHNESS AND SUPERCOMPENSATION

F YOU GO to the gym and do a strength workout you apply stress to certain muscles. The short-term impact of this is that muscle tissue breaks down. If you follow your workout with a sufficient period of quality recovery, the muscles not only repair themselves but – in a process known as *supercompensation* – prepare for future stress by becoming stronger.

Stress + recovery = growth

The same is true for your nervous system and physiological processes. If you expose your system to stress, and then ensure that you get sufficient recovery, you will experience *adaptive toughening* – your physiology strengthens and becomes more resilient.

CHRONIC STRESS, RISK AVERSION AND SUSTAINED TRADING PERFORMANCE

Stress, as we have seen, has a metabolic demand, an energy requirement. The higher the level of stress, the more energy you burn. This is why intense and mentally stressful days in the markets feel physically tiring.

Below are the morning heart rate variability (HRV) readings of a trader experiencing three long and intense trading days. The first reading is close to his normal baseline; by the third day it is half of this. A reduction in HRV is indicative of strain on the nervous system, of increased stress, and/or fatigue. His physiology has been significantly impacted by the increased mental demands of trading longer and more intensely.

Day 1	14-hour day	HRV 53
Day 2	14-hour day	HRV 45
Day 3	14-hour day	HRV 26

It is important to balance the amount of energy going out of your system with the replenishment of those resources. The most important factor in *energy replenishment* is recovery, switching off and recharging.

To trade at your best and avoid the pitfalls of chronic stress it is critical to be mindful of the stress–recovery balance.

GETTING THE STRESS-RECOVERY BALANCE RIGHT

If you work out too much, too frequently or too intensely – and do not get sufficient recovery to balance the stress your muscles are under – you enter a phase of *overtraining*. Eventually the muscles become damaged and you risk getting injured.

But if you never workout – and spend all of your time 'recovering' – your muscles will not become stronger or conditioned to the stresses of working out.

Getting the balance of stress and recovery right is therefore essential for athletes to optimise their training. There is a whole science around recovery. The same is true for traders.

Stress + sufficient recovery = growth

Stress + insufficient recovery = breakdown

No stress + recovery = no growth

Below are two physiological profiles of traders taken over a three-day period. The resources line – the trend line – shows the in and out flows of energy into their system. Stress depletes, recovery restores.

Trader A has a positive stress–recovery balance. You can see how, over the three-day period, his resources are not only restored but actually *increased*.

By contrast, trader B has a negative stress–recovery balance; his resources are reduced over the three-day period.

TRADER A

TRADER B

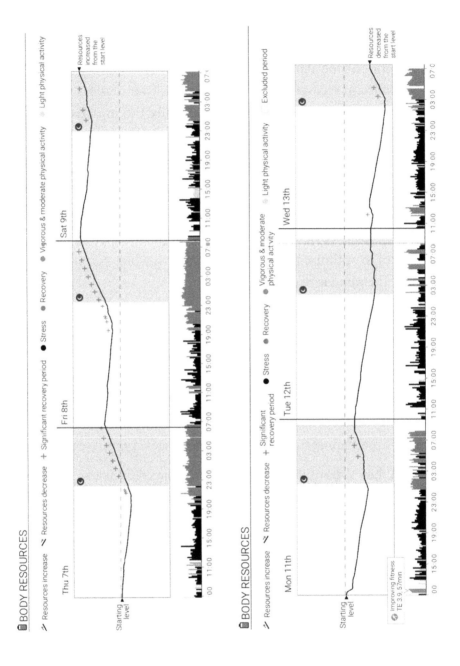

When the stress–recovery balance is right, traders optimise their physiological state and enhance their decision-making potential. They are also able to benefit from the adaptive responses to stress, avoid chronic stress and sustain performance over time.

Research from Firstbeat (firstbeat.com) in Finland – a company born out of the Finnish Olympic Institute, which provides physiological data and analysis to elite athletes and teams, healthcare providers, corporations and wearable tech manufacturers – suggests that the 'right' amount of recovery on a daily basis is 30% for "normal people, under normal conditions".

If you are getting 7–8 hours of good quality sleep per day, then you will not be far off that number. However, many of my trading clients are not sleeping long enough or well enough to achieve close to 30%. Many of them are consistently in a state of *underrecovery*.

WHAT IS RECOVERY?

Following a period of intense trading activity, a trader I was coaching decided to take a break to recover and recharge before returning to the markets. During this period I was conducting some research at the firm he traded with. A number of its traders, including this one, were collecting physiological data on a daily basis so that we could assess the impact of trading the markets on their physiology and the impact of their physiology on trading the markets.

Following a period of intense trading with high stress and high fatigue we could see that this trader's daily HRV reading decreased – as would be expected. For his recovery break, the trader went on a short skiing break with some of his friends. When I received his data it was very interesting to see that during the course of his four days on the slopes (and with the après-ski activity that followed) his HRV numbers had continued to fall.

He was not recovering. In fact, his physiology was further declining.

Given the exertion of several hours skiing per day, increased alcohol consumption and late nights, this was not unexpected. While this 'break' had been enjoyable – and felt like a rest – it was not recovery. It had been mentally refreshing; extremely diverting; a pleasant and much-needed change of scenery.

Depletion in action

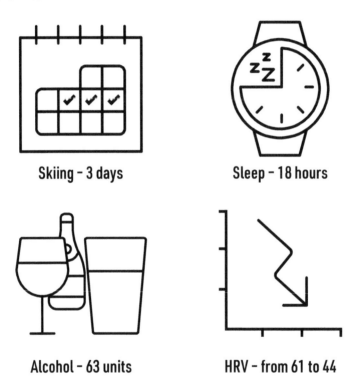

Skiing – 3 days

Sleep – 18 hours

Alcohol – 63 units

HRV – from 61 to 44

Recovery occurs when your body's nervous system switches into *parasympathetic mode*. The parasympathetic system is often referred to as 'rest and digest'. It is about putting the brakes on and slowing down.

Physiologically:

- your heart rate slows

- breathing becomes slower and deeper

- muscles relax

- blood flow returns to the digestive tract.

It is the opposite and antidote to the stress response, to fight or flight. It is the reverse of energising and switching on.

MEASURING STRESS AND RECOVERY

Historically we have measured recovery in very subjective ways:

- How recovered do you feel?

- How long did you sleep?

- How was the quality of your sleep?

- How did you relax/unwind during the course of the day?

Now, thanks to advances in technology and the use of heart-rate monitors and specific apps, we are able to capture physiological data that reflects a person's levels of stress and fatigue, primarily HRV.

I have conducted many physiological assessments and projects with my trading clients. Conducting these assessments allows traders to get objective data reflecting the quantity and level of stress they are under, the quantity and quality of their sleep, the quality and quantity of their recovery and the quality and quantity of their physical activity.

By examining the data we are able to gain insights in the stress–recovery balance, and how better to optimise stress management, sleep, recovery and physical activity to achieve high-performance physiological states.

Here's an in-depth look at one trader's experience:

Insights into a hedge fund trader's physiology

SWITCHING OFF TO SWITCH ON: RECOVERY STRATEGIES

In very simple performance terms, you need to be able to switch off so that you can switch on. It's the only way to ensure you have the physiological resources to trade at your best.

- How do you currently switch off? What are your recovery strategies?
- How is your sleep?
- Do you take recovery breaks during the trading day?
- What specific strategies (outside of sleep) do you utilise to put the brakes on, slow down, and restore?

Developing good recovery habits is fundamental to optimising your physiology, your resilience, and your trading performance.

SLEEP

Sleep is our prime source of recovery. It is one of our fundamental biological processes. The core reason for sleeping is to enable us to rest, recover and restore. Many traders I work with are not sleeping long enough or well enough, and they know it and can feel it.

The following diagrams show the sleep data of two different traders. Notice the difference in the sleep quantity and the quality between the two.

TRADER A

SLEEP

RESTORATIVE EFFECT OF SLEEP

100/100

60 - 100p Good
30 - 59p Moderate
0 - 29p Low

The sleep period was long enough and recovery was good.

LENGTH OF SLEEP — **8h 5min (Good)**
7h 35min

AMOUNT OF RECOVERY DURING SLEEP — 94%

< 50%   50 - 74%   ≥ 75%
Low   Moderate   Good

QUALITY OF RECOVERY (Heart rate variability) — **60 ms**

0 - 21 ms   22 - 41 ms   ≥ 42 ms
Low   Moderate   Good

SELF-REPORTED SLEEP QUALITY

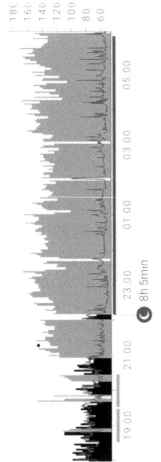

8h 5min

TRADER B

SLEEP

RESTORATIVE EFFECT OF SLEEP

24/100

60 - 100p Good
30 - 59p Moderate
0 - 29p Low

The sleep period was shorter than recommended and recovery was poor.

LENGTH OF SLEEP — **5h 40min (Moderate)**
2h 45min

AMOUNT OF RECOVERY DURING SLEEP — 49%

< 50%   50 - 74%   ≥ 75%
Low   Moderate   Good

QUALITY OF RECOVERY (Heart rate variability) — **15 ms**

0 - 19 ms   20 - 41 ms   ≥ 42 ms
Low   Moderate   Good

SELF-REPORTED SLEEP QUALITY

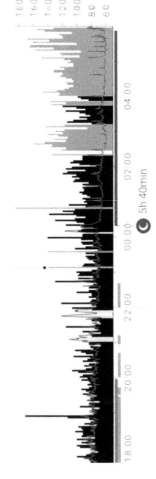

5h 40min

Sleep is not just important for recovery. It is also important for decision-making, risk-taking and performance. A study conducted at Duke University, North Carolina saw 29 young, healthy volunteers undertake a variety of gambling-based tasks while fully rested and then again following a night without sleep.[57] When the volunteers were rested, they demonstrated cautious patterns of gambling behaviour; with sleep deprivation, their risk perception shifted – and they became less sensitive to negative outcomes (losses) and put greater emphasis on positive outcomes (winning).

How is your sleep?

SATED Sleep Survey

		Rarely/ Never (0)	Sometimes (1)	Usually/ Always (2)
Satifaction	Are you satified with your sleep?			
Alertness	Do you stay awake all day without dozing?			
Timing	Are you asleep (or trying to sleep) between 2:00 and 4:00 a.m?			
Efficiency	Do you spend less than 30 minutes awake at night? (This includes the time it takes to fall asleep and awakenings from sleep.)			
Duration	Do you sleep between 6 and 8 hours per day?			

Source: National Institute of Health

In terms of sleeping well, there are a few basic *sleep hygiene* factors you should consider.

THE BEDROOM ENVIRONMENT

Goal: to create a bedroom environment conducive to sleeping well.

Make it:

- dark

- cool

- quiet

- technology-free.

THE WIND DOWN

Goal: to allow the body and brain to wind down; to slow down in preparation for sleep.

Achieve this by:

- being cautious about intensive exercise too close to bedtime

- being cautious about big meals in the wind-down period

- avoiding alcohol, which reduces sleep quality

- being mindful of caffeine intake – a stimulant with a half-life of six hours; consider having your last intake before noon

- being mindful of technology use – late-night tablet and phone use has been linked to a rise in reduced sleep quality; aim for a 30–60 minute tech-free window before bed

- meditation, breathing exercises, baths, showers – can all help you to unwind and prepare for sleep.

LIFESTYLE FACTORS

Goal: to build lifestyle practices that enable good sleep.

Achieve this through:

- consistent bed and waking time – shown to be a key factor in ensuring sleep quality
- physical activity – physical activity promotes good sleep quality.

CAN'T SLEEP?

Goal: to manage situations when you are having trouble sleeping.

Overcome this by:

- maintaining a bedside journal to make a note of any thoughts or worries keeping you awake
- practise mindfulness or breath-based strategies
- if you are in bed and awake for more than 20 minutes, get out of bed, read or do some other relaxing activity until you are tired; then return to bed when you are sleepy.

TACTICAL RECOVERY

"The mind must be given relaxation – it will rise improved and sharper after a good break. Just as rich fields must not be forced – for they will lose their fertility if never given a break – so constant work on the anvil will fracture the force of the mind. But it regains it powers if it is set free and relaxed a while. Constant work gives rise to a certain kind of dullness and feebleness in the rational soul."

– Seneca

Sleep is going to be your main source of recovery. The goal for traders who want to optimise their decision-making and performance should be to sleep as well as is possible. Bulletproof traders are those who prioritise sleep as *the* key recovery strategy and as a key performance enhancer.

But there are other sources of recovery outside of sleep. This is known as *tactical recovery* – something I have done a lot work on with my clients.

Many traders spend long periods of time sat at their desks. This may be necessary, especially during busy market periods. However, it is important to recognise that it is hard for the brain and body to sustain high levels of focus and cognitive performance over extended periods of time.

In order to optimise performance, traders should consider alternating periods of focus and trading activity with periods of recovery – in what are known as *basic rest activity cycles* (BRAC).

In the rest periods you might consider getting away from screens, standing up, stretching and moving, hydrating, eating if required – and perhaps, if helpful, taking some time to put on the brakes through the use of a relaxation or breathing-based activity.

> "We should take wandering outdoor walks, so that the mind might be nourished and refreshed by the open air, and deep breathing."
>
> **– Seneca**

Examples of good tactical recovery strategies include:

- active recovery – walking, yoga, stretching
- passive recovery – breathing strategies, relaxation techniques, meditation, massage, naps.

24

DEVELOP YOUR PHYSIOLOGICAL FITNESS

PHYSICAL FITNESS AND STRESS RESILIENCE

Imagine doing a skydive for the first time. What would the experience be like?

A first-time parachute jump is stressful for most people, even those being trained by the military. Jumping out of an airplane and waiting for the chute to open and then gliding back to the ground elicits a strong physiological response.

It is stressful. For many people it gives rise to profound feelings of anxiety and fear.

However, that's not the whole story. A 2008 study measured the hormonal and cognitive response in novice sky divers.[58] And it found something that noticeably reduced stress and fear: physical fitness.

The research found that the skydivers with the lowest body fat levels experienced the least stress, as measured by their cortisol (stress hormone) levels. They also performed better on cognitive tests taken just before the jump. The fittest skydivers were the most physiologically and cognitively resilient.

When it comes to providing some resistance to the stress response, it appears that exercise and physical fitness play a key part.

PHYSICAL ACTIVITY AS STRESS MANAGEMENT

"For me the most important way to manage my trading stress is exercise. I have in the past let trading take over my life and kept my eyes on the screens for all hours of the day, but the end result is never good. It needs to be built into my routine as it's very hard when I start to break the routine to get back on track with exercise – but it really does help clear my mind and the feeling I get after a good workout helps lift my mood after the worst of days."

– An investment bank trader

Many of my trading clients use physical activity to manage their stress levels.

The activation of the stress response in the body energises it, releasing adrenaline and hormones such as cortisol into the system. These are helpful and play a key role in the short term. In a situation of physical threat or challenge – if you have to fight or fly – this energy would be utilised and depleted. Once the threat or challenge is over, the recovery process would see them replenished. Homeostasis – the body's default physiological setting – is restored.

But traders are not actually facing physical fight or flight. They are not using the energy of the stress response to move the body. They are sitting in front of a screen, often for long periods.

When you take part in physical activity, even a walk, you give your body a chance to utilise the energy in your system. You let it wash out the stress hormones. You allow the body to reset.

On top of this, when exercise is more intense, there is also the release of endorphins – which can promote feelings of positivity and wellbeing, changing your mood.

> "Exercise is the best for managing my stress – either lifting weights or riding horses. Nothing like shovelling a bunch of horse manure in the barn or brushing dirt off an animal to take me out of the abstract world. Cleaning out closets or the garage is very therapeutic for me, too, and so is gardening. Digging in the dirt and planting flowers makes me happy."
>
> **– A hedge fund trader**

How much physical activity do you need to do? The general consensus among national health associations is at least 150 minutes of moderate-intensity activity, or 75 minutes of vigorous activity, per week.

That's 30 minutes per day, five days a week of moderate-intensity activity.

The data from my physiological tests of trader clients showed that:

- 65% of traders felt that they were doing enough physical activity to get health benefits

- but the objective physiological monitoring showed that only 24% actually were.

That is to say, 76% of traders were *not* doing enough physical activity to achieve basic health promotion – or the performance-enhancing benefits of moving and exercising.

Reported vs. measured activity

👤 Self-reported physical activity

65% Feel that they are physically active enough to get health benefits

📊 Measured physical activity

24% Were physically active enough to get health benefits

45% Were moderately physically active

31% Were not physically active enough

TRAINING PHYSIOLOGICAL RESILIENCE

Exercise and developing physical fitness are not the only ways to build physiological resilience.

Between June and July 2007, I conducted a study with 19 London-based proprietary traders to assess the effectiveness of a specific physiological state known as *coherence* on their trading performance.

Coherence is a psychophysiological state that can be tracked using heart rate variability (HRV) data. At times when we are stressed, anxious, frustrated or angry the heart receives conflicting signals from the nervous system. The plot of HRV appears jagged and disordered. The electrical signal the heart is generating is said to be chaotic.

The alternative electrical signal produced by the heart is one of coherence. This occurs when the cardiovascular system is operating efficiently and is in balance with the nervous system. When a coherent state is reached, HRV appears smooth and regular.

Being in a state of coherence has been shown to improve cognitive function, enhance memory, decision-making, creativity, perceptual clarity, behaviour and performance – while at the same time reducing the impact of excessive stress and pressure, and improving wellbeing.

Chaotic and coherent heart rhythms

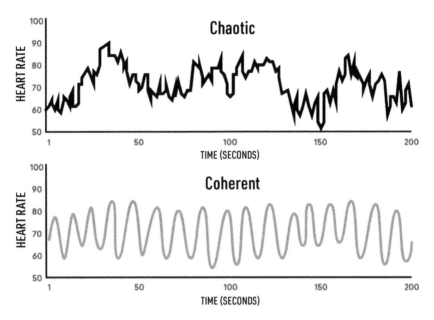

Source: www.heartmath.org

My clients completed some baseline psychometric and self-assessment reports and received a half-day of behavioural training. Here they learned about their physiology, how it impacted on their trading decision-making and performance, and were taught techniques for achieving a state of coherence.

During the six-week study period, traders were asked to practise the techniques – with a strategic daily 10-minute practice, then the use of shorter tactical techniques as required in the moment. When the study period finished, they performed the baseline tests again, and the pre- and post-data was analysed.

Following the physiological training, results showed that traders experienced lower levels of stress, fatigue, anxiety, anger and frustration; and higher levels of relaxation, motivation and focus. They felt more in control and were more decisive.

There was also an interesting impact on the traders' sleep, with 47% rating their sleep as inadequate before the study and only 14% rating it as inadequate post.

Trader physiological training – pre- and post-responses

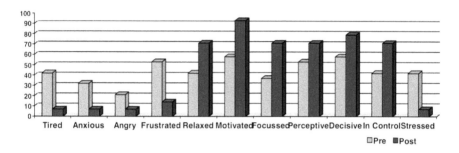

Training your physiological state provides a dual benefit. It can be used to counteract the effects of pressure or negative emotions in the immediate moment, as well as provide long-term benefits through rebuilding the body's natural energy reserves. The result is substantially enhanced feelings of wellbeing, energy and confidence – as well as improving personal health and resilience. All of which help you to perform.

Here is a heart-focused breathing technique.

What it does:

- Creates coherence, balances your nervous system, activates your pre-frontal cortex (executive function in the brain, for decision-making, planning, strategising, long-term thinking, self-regulation, task focus).

- Reduces stress reactivity – shifts the hormonal balance, including adrenaline and cortisol.

- Shifts the experience of negative emotional states to a more neutral one.

- Promotes homeostasis – the body's biological balance point.

How to do it:

- Focus your attention on to the area of your heart – get out of your head, and focus your attention in the body.

- Breathe a little slower and deeper than usual, in a smooth and sustained rhythm; try breathing for five seconds in, and five seconds out.

- Breathe in and out through the nose – it's more effective and efficient – and with a relaxed diaphragm/belly.

When to do it:

- In moments you feel stressed – take a few 5–5 breaths.

- Throughout the day in short doses – as a 'recharge'; perhaps 60 seconds at a time, or six times through the 5–5 breathing pattern.

- Before key decision moments or market events to get into a coherent high-performance state – perhaps for two to five minutes.

- As recovery – if you are feeling stressed or experiencing extreme emotions following a loss, making a mistake or any other adverse event, it can be useful to re-balance your physiology before attempting to think or act your way out of the situation. Practise the coherent breathing until you can noticeably feel that your state has shifted.

- Daily, as a training practice to develop your body's ability to achieve and sustain coherence, to develop your physiological fitness. A good first target is five minutes per day, perhaps building to ten minutes per day.

TRADING WELL

At the core of all high performance is wellbeing. It is hard to do anything at your best if you are not mentally, emotionally and physically well. The old adage of 'healthy body, healthy mind' is true. Since the jogging revolution of the 1970s there has been an increasing interest and focus on physical health and wellbeing. That focus has, more recently, expanded to include people's mental health.

Of course, as we know, the mind and body are not two discrete entities. They are deeply entwined, and both mind and body play a key role in the performance of any craft – how well you trade, the decisions you make, and how effectively you deal with the consequences of those decisions.

Bulletproof traders are those that prioritise their wellbeing.

> "I feel the key to managing my stress is via energy management. This has become a huge thing for me. I am very mindful of my energy management now; I try to manage it as best as possible. When I don't manage it well – I am mindful of it. I trade and act accordingly."
>
> **– An equities trader**

I always encourage my clients to consider the importance of their wellbeing. It's about *trading well*. That means trading in a well state, as much as it means good performance. The latter is, in the long run, impossible without the former. Wellbeing can be thought of as the platform on which your trading is built:

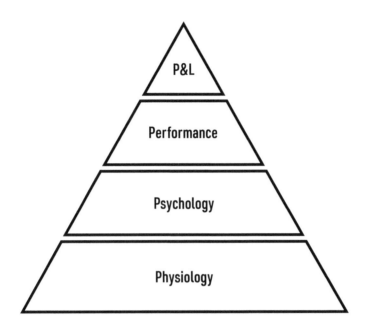

THE PHYSIOLOGICAL PLATFORM

One successful fund manager I spoke to listed a variety of different approaches he employed to help him deal with the stresses and challenges of trading the markets:

- physical exercise
- sleep
- breathing exercises
- mental rehearsal and visualisation
- meditation.

Meditation, mindfulness and yoga have all become increasingly popular practices for helping traders to manage the stresses and strains of trading, and to optimise their performance. The use of such approaches is growing in many performance-orientated areas, including sports, the military, law enforcement, trauma medicine and in corporate leadership programmes.

Finding 8–12 minutes per day to undertake in some kind of meditation or mindfulness practice can help reduce your stress reactivity, improve your emotional regulation, manage your difficult thoughts more effectively, make you less impulsive and enhance your overall health and wellbeing.

> "Meditation has become a huge part of my day – meditating at roughly 9am each morning and then, where possible, at 3.45pm. I often use methods learned in meditation when I feel myself becoming stressed and being pulled out of balance."
>
> – A proprietary trader

The awareness of such wellbeing practices and their impact on trading performance is not new. I once received a copy of Jesse Livermore's *How to Trade in Stocks* from a fund manager client, with whom I had conduced a series of physiological assessments (including while being on holiday, and still watching the markets). He left a post-it note marking a particular page and paragraph:

> "The following rule is a rule I developed from a great trader: Keep stress at bay – act in all ways to keep the mind clear and your judgement correct. I did all I could to achieve this in my physical life by going to bed early, eating and drinking lightly, taking exercise, standing upright at the stock ticker, standing while on the telephone and demanding silence in the office."[59]

This book was published in 1940.

I think of these types of behaviours and habits as a trader's *performance lifestyle*. They're the factors, often outside of trading hours, that contribute to their wellbeing and performance. The Stoics were well aware of the importance of looking after the body to enhance the mind, and the importance of wellbeing to living a good life.

"Wellbeing is realised by small steps, but it is truly no small thing."

– Zeno

One of the risks that traders face, especially those operating at the higher-frequency end, is that of exhaustion and even burnout. By recognising burnout as a potential occupational hazard, we can take preventive measures, including:

- keeping expectations realistic
- getting time away from screens
- prioritising recovery
- engaging in enjoyable activities.

CONCLUSION

25

THE END - AND
A BEGINNING

I HOPE THAT READING this book will have given you some knowledge, insights and actions you can take and integrate into your own trading. I hope that it will help you manage the stresses, challenges and demands of trading the markets more effectively.

Here are some reminders of the key principles and practices.

- **Getting good at the downs:** Trading requires taking risk under conditions of uncertainty, novelty and uncontrollability. There will be stresses, challenges and difficulties. These are a part of the trading experience. The goal is not to avoid them, but rather to get good at them.

- **Bulletproof mindset:** Your mindset – how you think about trading, the markets, risk, uncertainty – impacts how you feel and behave. Be mindful of your beliefs and perceptions. Which are useful? Which are not useful?

- **Stress mindset:** Seeing stress as helpful can have a positive impact on both your long-term health and your short-term performance.

- **Blackbox thinking:** It is helpful to think about mistakes, losses and setbacks as opportunities; a chance to get feedback, to learn, develop and become more resilient.

- **Commitment:** What are the specific actions that you need to take that will maximise your chances of success? What strengths and qualities (values) do you want to demonstrate in your trading? What is important to you?

- **Manage your risk:** Manage your risk, aiming to balance opportunity maximisation with decision-making quality; position size with competence, context and risk tolerance.

- **Embrace uncertainty:** Uncertainty is inherent in trading – embrace it. Build a mindset of impermanence, and, where you can, use the strategy of planned uncertainty.

- **Plan for the worst:** Use a pre-mortem to help you plan for the worst, and decide on what action you will take – if-then – if it should occur.

- **Present moment:** Develop the skill of present-moment attention so that you can stay task/process-focused, market-focused and keep awareness of your internal experience.

- **Process:** Focus on making good trading decisions, getting better at making trading decisions and developing a strong trading process.

- **Control:** Control the controllables. Identify what you can and cannot control in your trading. Focus on what is controllable. Take responsibility for how you respond.

- **Willingness:** Get comfortable with being uncomfortable. Accept discomfort as a part of the trading experience, and develop your willingness to experience it in the service of achieving your trading goals.

- **Unhooking:** Build awareness of your thoughts and the narratives you tell yourself about trading. Learn to unhook from unhelpful thoughts. Stay focused on action.

- **Emotions:** Learn to work with, not avoid or control, your emotions. Bring awareness to how you are feeling: notice it, name it. Think about emotions as data and how you might be able to harness them.

- **Confidence:** Build your confidence in dealing with difficult trading situations – strengths, challenges overcome, support? Build up your poker-chip pile.

- **Composure:** Develop your ability to stay calm in difficult and stressful market moments. Competence, preparation and state management are the foundation. Breathwork is an effective strategy to regulate your state in the moment.

- **Compassion:** Beating yourself up too hard and too much erodes confidence. Develop the ability to balance your inner critic with a compassionate coach. Be mindful of judging versus describing.

- **Mental flexibility:** Practise seeing situations from different perspectives. Find the opportunity in the difficult. Take a high view. What would a role model do?

- **Behavioural flexibility:** Build the capacity to both flex in the short term, and adapt in the long term, to adjust your process and strategy to meet market environments.

- **State monitoring:** Develop a process for monitoring your physiological state – stress and fatigue levels. It could be subjective, or objective using HRV data collection and analysis.

- **Recovery:** Getting the stress recovery balance right is key to building stress resilience and to sustaining high-performance trading. Focus on getting good quality sleep, and develop ways to relax and switch off so that you can switch *on*.

- **Physiological fitness:** There are many ways in which you can train your physiology to be more resilient to stress and the challenges and demands of trading the markets. Consider your habits around physical wellbeing, activity and health. Train for coherence. Use mindfulness-based mind-fitness training.

I'll leave you with three keys to using all of the above:

1. imagination

2. action

3. support.

1. IMAGINE YOUR FUTURE

Get, and keep, a clear vision in your mind of what you're working towards through all this.

Imagine a future you: a more resilient trader, capable of handling the demands you face in trading the markets, and overcoming challenges with aplomb.

- What would be different?

- What would you notice?

- What action would you be taking?

- How would you be feeling?

- What thoughts would you have?

- Where are the opportunities for you to develop, to become a mentally stronger, more robust, composed and resilient trader than you currently are?

2. TAKING ACTION

Resilience, toughness, hardiness are all developed – forged. Your inner citadel is built not through reading and knowledge, but through application, practice and experience.

So take action.

> "That's why the philosophers warn us not to be satisfied with mere learning, but to add practice and then training. For as time passes we forget what we learned and end up doing the opposite, and hold opinions the opposite of what we should."
>
> **– Epictetus**

Each moment of challenge, difficulty and stress the market offers you is an immediate opportunity to practise your bulletproofing skills.

- What action will you take?

- When will you take it?

- How will it help you?

Trading challenge	Current approach, skills	Bulletproof knowledge and skills to apply

3. SUPPORT

I hope you benefit from reading this book and that it can play some small part in helping you to trade at your best and achieve your trading potential.

If you have any questions or feedback please feel free to get in touch via my website or drop me an email.

Best wishes,

Steve

steve@performanceedgeconsulting.co.uk

www.performanceedgeconsulting.co.uk

ACKNOWLEDGEMENTS

This is my fourth book covering the topic of trading, investing and betting psychology and performance. Each of these books has been a challenge in different ways, and there are always highs and lows in the writing process, as in life. None of them could have been written without the support and input of a number of people, and these pages are to briefly acknowledge and thank them.

They say that charity begins at home – well, so do the thank you's. Writing a book is a time-consuming, energy-sapping process, and that time and energy are given to the book sometimes at the expense of the family, the home. My wife Sabine, and two boys Oliver (O.J.) and Casper (Caz) have been, as always, very supportive and understanding throughout the writing process. I have been fortunate to some extent that Netflix, the Xbox and YouTube have given them other ways to enjoy their time while I have been writing, and this has somewhat reduced my feelings of guilt about not being with them.

There were a number of traders who I reached out to for input with this book – from banks, hedge funds, asset managers, commodities trading houses, proprietary trading groups, and utilities companies. Many of them took valuable time out of the markets and life to respond. You will have seen their input throughout the book most clearly in their quotes I used, and more subtly in the tone of the book and the topic choice. As agreed with them, I have respected their anonymity, but it is important to me to let them know how much I appreciate their contribution. You will know who you are – a huge thank you.

This book is a reflection of 15 years of working with thousands of different traders across the globe. Every workshop I have delivered, every coaching session I have had with a client, and every piece of assessment work or consulting work I have conducted, has in some way contributed to my own thinking and doing, and to the content that has appeared in this book. So, a big thank you to all of the clients that I have worked for giving me the opportunity to work with you, and for informing my work so much.

There are three core pillars on which this book is predominantly built – acceptance and commitment coaching (therapy), human physiology and Stoic philosophy. Three fascinating areas, each with their own theories, models and frameworks. The knowledge, insight, techniques and strategies in this book draw on the work of many accomplished and renowned people and institutions. To those who did the research, developed the frameworks, and enabled me to use their findings to benefit my clients and the readers of this book – a big thank you for your work and a hat tip to your dedication to the mastery of your craft.

Finally, I am not sure how publishers view authors, and whether I am typical of other authors or not, but I can imagine that it must be a job that is quite frustrating and difficult at times – one that I am sure requires its own level of bulletproofing. I have had the pleasure of writing three books now with the team at Harriman House, and I just wanted to say again, thank you for giving me the opportunity to write this book, and a special shout out to Christopher Parker, the editor, for his support in shaping the content of the book, his patience during the writing process and the immense amount of effort he spent in editing this book such that it became what we both hope is the 'best version of the book' for the reader.

ENDNOTES

1   *The Mindful and Effective Employee: An Acceptance and Commitment Therapy Training Manual For Improving Well-Being and Performance;* Frank Bond, Paul Flaxman, Fredrik Livheim, New Harbinger, 2013.

2   *The Hardy Executive: Health Under Stress;* Burr Ridge, IL. Maddi, S. and Kobasa, S, Irwin Publishing, 1984.

3   *Developing Mental Toughness: Coaching Strategies To Improve Performance, Resilience and Wellbeing;* Doug Strycharczyk, Peter Clough, Kogan Page, 2015.

4   *The Obstacle is the Way*, Ryan Holiday, Profile Books, 2014.

5   www.si.com/nfl/2015/12/08/ryan-holiday-nfl-stoicism-book-pete-carroll-bill-belichick

6   *Behavioural Investing: A Practitioner's Guide to Applying Behavioural Finance;* James Montier, John Wiley and Sons, 2007.

7   www.dragondoor.com/build_your_inner_citadel

8   *The Little Book of Stoicism: Timeless Wisdom to Gain Resilience, Confidence and Calmness;* Jonas Salzgeber, 2019 (www.njlifehacks.com).

9   *The Upside of Stress: Why Stress is Good for You (And How to Get Good at it)*; Kelly McGonigal, Penguin/Random House, 2015.

10   *Black Box Thinking: The Surprising Truth About Success*; Matthew Syed, John Murray, 2015.

11   *Principles: Life And Work*; Ray Dalio, Simon & Schuster, 2017.

12   dailystoic.com/stoicism-for-athletes

13   *The Psychology of Enhancing Human Performance: The Mindfulness-Acceptance-Commitment (MAC) Approach*; Frank L. Gardner and Zella E. Moore, Springer Publishing Company, 2007.

14   *Acceptance and Commitment Therapy: 100 Key Points and Techniques*; Richard Bennett and Joseph E. Oliver, Routledge, 2019.

15   *The Mindful and Effective Employee: An Acceptance and Commitment Therapy Training Manual For Improving Well-Being and Performance;* Frank Bond, Paul Flaxman, Fredrik Livheim, New Harbinger, 2013, p.25.

16   *Ibid.,* p.26.

17   www.ncbi.nlm.nih.gov/pubmed/24405362

18   *The Road To Excellence: The Acquisition Of Expert Performance in the Arts and Sciences, Sports and Games*; K. Anders Ericsson, Lawrence Erlbaum Associates Inc, 1996.

19   www.ncbi.nlm.nih.gov/pmc/articles/PMC3410434; *Mind over Matter: Reappraising Arousal Improves Cardiovascular and Cognitive Responses to Stress*; Jeremy P. Jamieson, Matthew K. Nock, and Wendy Berry Mendes; *J Exp Psychol Gen.* 2012 Aug; 141(3): 417–422. (In *The Upside of Stress – Why Stress is Good for You (And How to Get Good at it)*; Kelly McGonigal, Penguin/Random House, 2015.)

20   Steve Clark, Omni Global Fund, in *Hedge Fund Market Wizards: How Winning Traders Win*; Jack Schwager, John Wiley and Sons, 2012.

21   Joe Vidich, Manalapan Fund, in *Ibid.*

22   *Ibid.*, p.490.

23   *Trading In The Zone: Master The Market With Confidence, Discipline And A Winning Attitude*; Mark Douglas, New York Institute of Finance, 2000.

24 www.forbes.com/sites/alicegwalton/2016/03/29/uncertainty-about-the-future-is-more-stressful-than-knowing-that-the-future-is-going-to-suck/ *Origin Nature Communications* journal

25 dailystoic.com/embrace-the-uncertainty

26 dailystoic.com/premortem

27 *Back to the Future: Temporal Perspective in the Explanation of Events', Journal of Behavioral Decision Making*, Vol. 2, No. 1, January/March 1989, 25–38, Deborah J. Mitchell, J. Edward Russo, and Nancy Pennington

28 *Winning Decisions: Getting it Right the First Time;* J. Edward Russo and Paul J. H. Schoemaker, (New York: Currency, 2002), 111–112.

29 *The Attention Revolution: Unlocking The Power of The Focused Mind;* B. Alan Wallace, Wisdom Publications, U.S., 1st Wisdom edition (2006).

30 oro.open.ac.uk/34544/1/Final%20report%20-%20publishable%20format.pdf

31 *Self-Awareness: The Hidden Driver of Success and Satisfaction;* Travis Bradberry, Perigee Trade, 2009.

32 Quoted in *Your Brain At Work: Strategies For Overcoming Distraction, Regaining Focus and Working Smarter All Day Long;* David Rock, HarperCollins, London, 2009.

33 *Super Trader: Make Consistent Profits In Good and Bad Markets;* Van K. Tharp, McGraw-Hill, New York, 2011.

34 *Ibid.*

35 *Accounting for the Effects of Accountability;* J.S. Lerner and P.E. Tetlock, *Psychological Bulletin* 125 (1999) 255–27.

36 *Winning Decisions: Getting it Right the First Time*, J. Edward Russo and Paul J. H . Schoemaker, Currency; 1st edition, 2001.

37   *The Hour Between Dog and Wolf: Risk-Taking, Gut Feeling and the Biology of Boom and Bust*; John Coates, Fourth Estate, 2012.

38   *The Hardy Executive: Health Under Stress*; Maddi, S. and Kobasa, S., Irwin Publishing, Burr Ridge, IL., 1984.

39   *Man's Search For Meaning: The Classic Tribute to Hope from the Holocaust*; Viktor E. Frankl, Rider, New edition, 2004.

40   'The Psychophysiology of Real Time Financial Risk Processing', *Journal of Cognitive Neuroscience*, 14(3), 323–339; Lo, A.W. and Repin, D.V. 2002.

41   *White Bears And Other Unwanted Thoughts: Suppression, Obsession and The Psychology of Mental Control*; Daniel M. Wegner, Guilford Press; 1st edition, 24 May 1994.

42   www.nature.com/articles/srep32986

43   oro.open.ac.uk/34544/1/Final%20report%20-%20publishable%20format.pdf

44   www.sekoyta.com/tribe

45   UCSD Center For Mindfulness, mPEAK programme.

46   *The Upside of Stress: Why Stress is Good for You (And How To Get Good at it)*; Kelly McGonigal, Penguin/Random House, 2015, p.113.

47   *The Confidence Gap: From Fear to Freedom*; Dr Russ Harris, Robinson, 2019.

48   *The Mindful Athlete: Secrets to Pure Performance*; George Mumford, Parallax Press, 2015.

49   Power Speed Endurance – powerspeedendurance.com/breathing

50   *Self-Compassion: Stop Beating Yourself Up and Leave Insecurity Behind*; Kristin Neff, Yellow Kite, 2011.

51   www.psychologytoday.com/gb/articles/200306/our-brains-negative-bias

52 medium.com/stoicism-philosophy-as-a-way-of-life/take-a-view-from-above-d24d423f978a

53 *Floored*, James Allen-Smith, 2009.

54 *Change or Die: The Three Keys to Change in Work and Life;* Alan Deutschman, HarperBusiness, Reprint edition, 2007.

55 *The Talent Lab: How to Turn Potential into World Beating Success;* Owen Slot, Simon Timson, Ebury Press, 2018.

56 Danziger, S., Levav, J. and Avnaim-Pesso, L. (2011). 'Extraneous factors in judicial decisions'. Proceedings of the National Academy of Sciences USA, 108(17), 6889–6892.

57 corporate.dukehealth.org/news-listing/sleep-deprived-people-make-risky-decisions-based-too-much-optimism

58 *Extreme Fear: The Science of Your Mind in Danger,* Jeff Wise, Palgrave Macmillan, 2010.

59 *How to Trade in Stocks: The Classic Formula for Understanding Timing, Money Management and Emotional Control;* Jesse Livermore, McGraw-Hill Education, 2006.

Milton Keynes UK
Ingram Content Group UK Ltd.
UKHW020824110624
444009UK00006B/15